Architectural Design

Sensing the 21st-Century City:
Close-Up and Remote

Guest-edited by Brian McGrath and Grahame Shane

 **WILEY-ACADEMY**

Architectural Design
Vol 75 No 6 Nov/Dec 2005

Editorial Offices
International House
Ealing Broadway Centre
London W5 5DB
T: +44 (0)20 8326 3800
F: +44 (0)20 8326 3801
E: architecturaldesign@wiley.co.uk

Editor
Helen Castle

Design + Editorial Management
Mariangela Palazzi-Williams

Art Direction/Design
Christian Küsters (CHK Design)

Design Assistant
Hannah Dumphy (CHK Design)

**Project Coordinator
and Picture Editor**
Caroline Ellerby

Advertisement Sales
Faith Pidduck/Wayne Frost
01243 770254
fpidduck@wiley.co.uk

Editorial Board
Will Alsop, Denise Bratton, Adriaan
Beukers, André Chaszar, Peter Cook,
Teddy Cruz, Max Fordham, Massimiliano
Fuksas, Edwin Heathcote, Anthony Hunt,
Charles Jencks, Jan Kaplicky, Robert
Maxwell, Jayne Merkel, Monica Pidgeon,
Antoine Predock, Michael Rotondi, Leon
van Schaik, Ken Yeang

Contributing Editors
André Chaszar
Craig Kellogg
Jeremy Melvin
Jayne Merkel

ISBN-10 0470024186
Profile No 178

ISBN-13 9780470024188

Abbreviated positions:
b=bottom, c=centre, l=left, r=right

Front and back cover: Collage by
Emmanuel Pratt examining the mobile
phone as it influences sensory culture in
Johannesburg – 'Africa's New York City',
which is caught between first- vs third-
world notions of identity. © Emmanuel Pratt

AD
p 4 © Getty Images; pp 5(t) & 14-15(t) ©
Brian McGrath and Manolo F Ufer; p 5(b) ©
Martin/Baxi Architects; p 6 © Emmanuel
Pratt; p 7 © Grahame Shane; pp 8 & 9(r&tl)
© Rodrigo Guardia; p 9 (cl&bl) © Young-Jae
Oh; p 10 © Mary Cadenasso and STA Pickett;
p 11 USDA Forest Service, Space Imaging
LLC; p 12 © Justice Mapping Center with
the JFA Institute and the Spatial Design Lab,
GSAPP Columbia University; p 13 reprinted
with permission from Keyhole, www.key-
hole.com; p 15(b) © Manolo F Ufer; pp 16-17
© Mark Isarangkun na Ayuthaya; pp 18-19 &
21-3 © Christopher Small; p 20 © Space
Imaging; pp 24 & 25(tr&br) © Elisabeth
Blum; p 25(t) © Paulo Bastos Architect,
photo Consórcio JNS-HagaPlan/Fany
Cutcher Galender Architect; p 25(bl) © Paulo
Bastos Architect, photos Nelson Xavier
Architect; p 26 © The Baltimore Ecosystem
Study; pp 27-30 © Steffi Graham; p 31 ©
Erika Svendsen, Victoria Marshall and
Manolo F Ufer; pp 32-3 © Jan Leenknegt; pp
34-9 © Petia Morozov; pp 40 & 41(t) ©
Alessandro Cimini/Ignacio Lamar; p 41(b) ©
School of Architecture, Syracuse University;
pp 42-7 © Michael Batty and Andrew
Hudson-Smith + CASA/UCL; pp 48 & 49(b) ©
Antonio Scarponi, Stefano Massa, Federico
Pedrini, Barbara Galassi;
p 49(t) © Antonio Scarponi; p 50 © M
Pillhofer; pp 51-3, 54(t) & 55 © Hans Kiib
& Gitte Marling; p 54(b) © TRANSFORM/
Lars Bendrup; pp 56-7 © CITYSTUDIO, Els

Verbakel and Elie Derman; pp 58-63 © José
Echeverría, Jordi Mansilla and Jorge Perea;
pp 64 & 67-8 courtesy NASA/GSFC/METI/
ERSDAC/JAROS & US/Japan ASTER Science
Team; pp 65-6 © Satya Pemmaraju; p 69
courtesy NLR Remote Sensing; pp 70-1 ©
Krystina A Kaza; pp 73-4 © Geoffrey Rogers;
p 75 © May Joseph; pp 76-9 © Martin/Baxi
Architects; pp 80-5 © Deborah Natsios; pp
86 & 87(t) © Sanjaya Hettiheka; p 87(b) ©
Jacques Descloitres, MODIS Rapid Response
Team, NASA/GSFC; p 87(c) © Eugènia Vidal;
pp 88-93 © Environmental Simulation Center
(ESC); pp 94(t) & 95(t&c) © Michele
Bertomen; p 94(b) © US Geological Survey;
p 95(bl) © Toxic Targeting, Inc.

AD+
pp 98 & 100(t) © www.dbox.com; p 100(b) ©
Gluckman Mayner Architects; p 101 © Ian
Schrager Company; pp 102, 105 (bl,tr&br)
& 106(tl) © Arup; p 104 © Richard Bryant,
arcaid.co.uk; p 105(tl) & 106(bl) © 2005
Álvaro Siza, Eduardo Souto de Moura with
Cecil Balmond, Arup; p 106(tr) © 2005 Álvaro
Siza; p 106(cr) © 2005 Eduardo Souto de
Moura; p 106(br) © Cecil Balmond, Arup;
pp 107-108 & 109(t) © Jonny Muirhead;
pp 109(b) & 110 © Foster and Partners;
pp 112-118 © Piercy Conner Ltd; p 119 ©
Ross Cunningham/Piercy Conner; p 120 ©
Victoria Watson; p 122 © William McLean;
pp 124-126 © Edward Denison.

Subscription Offices UK
John Wiley & Sons Ltd.
Journals Administration Department
1 Oldlands Way, Bognor Regis
West Sussex, PO22 9SA
T: +44 (0)1243 843272
F: +44 (0)1243 843232
E: cs-journals@wiley.co.uk

Printed in Italy by Conti Tipicolor.
All prices are subject to change
without notice.
[ISSN: 0003-8504]

AD is published bimonthly and is available
to purchase on both a subscription basis
and as individual volumes at the following
prices.

Single Issues
Single issues UK: £22.50
Singles issues outside UK: US$45.00
Details of postage and packing charges
available on request.

Annual Subscription Rates 2005
Institutional Rate
Print only or Online only: UK£175/US$290
Combined Print and Online: UK£193/US$320
Personal Rate
Print only: UK£99/US$155
Student Rate
Print only: UK£70/US$110

Prices are for six issues and include
postage and handling charges. Periodicals
postage paid at Jamaica, NY 11431. Air
freight and mailing in the USA by
Publications Expediting Services Inc, 200
Meacham Avenue, Elmont, NY 11003

Individual rate subscriptions must be paid
by personal cheque or credit card.
Individual rate subscriptions may not be
resold or used as library copies.

Postmaster
Send address changes to AD Publications
Expediting Services, 200 Meacham Avenue,
Elmont, NY 11003

Sensing the 21st-Century City:
Close-Up and Remote
Guest-edited by Brian McGrath and Grahame Shane

The instability of the environment and associated virulent freak weather conditions threaten economic and political stability at a local and global scale. Here, the cloud before the storm: the Gulf coast braces for Hurricane Katrina.

'Uncertainty stems from the fact that the benefits of globalisation will not be universal, and conflict, instability, environmental and ethical issues will rise to the fore even more.' When Brian McGrath and Grahame Shane wrote these words in their introduction in the early summer of 2005, little could they have anticipated just how cruelly apt they would prove to be by the issue's publication in the autumn. Since then, the ravages that Hurricane Katrina has left in her wake have almost incessantly been played out on our TV screens, catapulting the world's population to a heightened awareness of the earth's precarious environmental position and the fragility of the general urban situation. Following close on the heels of the tsunami in the Pacific Ocean, Katrina has confronted us with the very human misery that is brought about by a natural disaster on any side of the world. She has also effectively transmitted into everyone's living rooms the images of a third-world urban population in a supposedly first-world country: an impoverished people, left at starvation point; desolation and desperation fanning up violence and lawlessness; statistical knowledge of the widening gap between rich and poor; and the promise of a potentially volatile situation being very different from the 'in-your face' experiential power of TV footage. The poignancy of this issue cannot thus be ignored in light of recent events. It is unarguable that remote sensing and hand-held devices will, in the future, play a very important part in the surveillance and monitoring of environmental and demographic shifts in conurbations. They will have an important role in both the pre-empting of natural disasters and immediate warning systems. (After the tsunami, there was media discussion about how mobile phones might be used to give out warning in the effected area.) In the States, it is certain that there will be a call for further investment in technology to better anticipate the enormity of such extreme weather conditions and to test man-made defences. However, what McGrath and Shane, as architects and urban designers, have brought to this context is that technology alone is not enough. This issue combines penetrating essays with what is effectively a scrapbook of localised global reports compiled through the guest-editors' own academic international network. It stresses, as they describe, both an understanding of the 'near and the far', and technology analytically interpreted on the ground with the aid of intelligence, creativity and humanity. ⌀

The streets of Johannesburg and courtyards of Aranya are inundated with fresh faces and new voices from satellite TVs and mobile phones. Broadband fuels teenage fantasies in Seoul's cyber-bangs and connects call centres in Bangalore. Along scenic parkways outside Washington DC, snapshots of GPS-guided tours are transmitted to family back in Sri Lanka, while suburban beltway Muslims are targeted as terrorist suspects. Such are some of the vantage points presented in this special issue of ⌂.

Telecommunications and surveillance have penetrated every corner of the world, but the breathtaking satellite images often used to picture our urbanised planet give no indication of the diversity of social exchange that is percolating on the ground. This century, the hierarchical networked global city model will be increasingly altered by broader participation in world culture and the global economy. The flattening of the network city into global meshworks will not result in cultural homogenisation, but in the emergence of a new heterogeneous urban landscape.

While the US National Intelligence Commission (NIC) concedes the important role of China and India in the 21st century, Janet Abu-Lughod has shown that these 'new players' were the key actors during the 15th century, when 'India was on the way to everywhere'.[1] Thinking of cities as networks of relationships began with Ferdinand Braudel's studies of Mediterranean trade, was developed further in Emmanuel Wallerstein's World-System analysis, extended in John Friedmann's World City hierarchy diagram, documented in detail by Peter Taylor, and transformed in Saskia Sassen's global city model of superimposed rich and poor components. The emerging meshwork city consists not only of technopoles and widespread networks that enable this global system to survive, but also of vast informal settlements housing over a third of the world's population. These variations are not mutually exclusive. They can appear in simultaneous recombinations within a city, marking the era's particular urban signature, as hierarchical and distant systems are brought into greater contact via broadening access to information and cities.

The 21st-century global city, defined by the duality of mass urban migrations and continued exurban sprawl, provides innumerable challenges and opportunities for today's architects. Rapid environmental change requires scientific monitoring and management as forests and farmlands decline, coastlines flood as a result of global warming, vast informal settlements develop in the absence of master planning, and hypernodes monitor and influence everything through telecommunications, media, ecological assessments, foreign aid and military might. Close-up and remote devices are now being used, as never before, to shape and manage vast interconnected urban ecosystems at local, regional and global scales. Architects need to develop new technical, communication and networking skills in order to collaborate with scientists, decision makers and communities directly engaged with today's

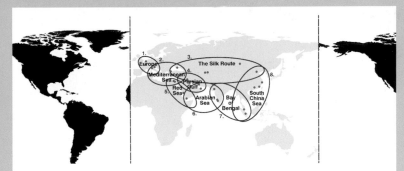

Janet Abu-Lughod describes the 15th-century world system in *Before European Hegemony* as eight overlapping arenas dominated by China and centred on India. The western hemisphere does not appear in this world system.

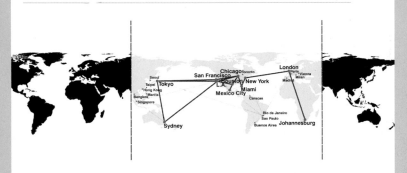

Peter Taylor's *World City Network* from 1985[2] reflects the Reagan/Thatcher era at the end of the Cold War. Here, global capitalism is a top-down system managed from New York, London and Tokyo through nodes such as São Paulo, Bangkok, Sydney and Johannesburg. China and India do not appear in this supposedly global network. (Maps redrawn by Manolo F Ufer)

Kadambari Baxi and Reinhold Martin's characterisation of the current phase of globalisation as continuous circuits. Their repetitive rendering of the globe is similar to Andy Warhol's multiple portraits of Marilyn Monroe. Pop repetition flattens the iconic singular image, anticipating *New York Times* columnist Thomas Friedman's pronouncement after returning from Bangalore that the world is flat.

challenges. Remote sensing and hand-held devices can be combined to create just-in-time delivery of design and planning services by collapsing the near and the far.

In the film *2 or 3 Things I Know about Her* (1967), Jean-Luc Godard describes the huge societal mutation of a modernising Paris by attempting to get very close to one individual. As we examine new cities formed by new technologies in a new millennium, the question Godard continually asks himself in the film can be redirected to today's urbanists: 'Am I watching from too far or too close?'

Today, the city of Johannesburg lies at the crux of a very unique transition of urban growth and development. Since being selected to host the soccer world cup in 2010, Johannesburg finds itself caught in the midst of rapidly redefining its apartheid-torn history into its 'proudly South African' global aspirations of becoming a 'world-class African city'. Jozi has become a city that often finds itself plagued by a symptomatic first-/third-world schizophrenic sense of identity, a never-ending cycle of reproductions of global models of cultural identity and media representations spread between the likes of little Brazil, little Italy, little New York, little Paris, and so on.

As a result, the notion of 'image' has evoked a system of classification that attempts to ignore previously dominant racial subdivisions and assumes the character of a new societal 'pictionary', in so far as the recurring series of images in popular media have come to redefine a common record of 'way of being'. It is no wonder, therefore, that Joburg's inhabitants finds themselves struggling with the familiar dimension of the Hollywood-esque 'see to be seen' status-quo formula derived from the ensemble of (materiality + subjectivity)/(cell phone + digital gadgetry + luxury mobility) = POPULARITY STATUS. Inversely, however, the social division between the haves and have-nots becomes further stratified as such material objects of desire are double the cost of the US equivalent.

Meanwhile, it is difficult to imagine that, at one point in time, 80 per cent of the land and wealth of the country was dictated by a mere 13 per cent of the population.

With its rapid advancements in wireless networks and available technologies, Jozi has been hurled into a juxtaposed temporality of 'placelessness' typified by its gated communities and electric fencing down to the ever-growing independent, self-organising squatter camps. The influence of globalisation has become more a system of exchange, while capitalism acts as the motivator for the influx of media and defines the city's contemporary sense of culture. Nevertheless, it is essentially this same urban trap that delineates Johannesburg's own intrinsic sense of innovation and has spawned a culture that is conducive for new ideas and new ways of doing things.

In its continual attempts to replicate and redefine its city form/image, Johannesburg, often referred to as 'the New York City of Africa', has undergone a cyclical process of identity creation that is linked symptomatically to the behaviour of global investments and international media influences such as film, television and radio. The image on the left depicts the remote clash of overtly Western-influenced imagery/programming represented during the course of daily TV broadcasts with an overlay of text depicting select statistics that chart Johannesburg's development as an industrial metropolis. The image on the right examines more of the sensory influences of cellular culture in this highly dynamic contrast between suburban vs inner-city social conditions that redefines Johannesburg's phenomena of twin (first- vs third-world) notions of identity.

Modelling the 21st-Century City

There are two opposing interpretations of the new global city, based on United Nations (UN) and World Bank data. In *Mapping the Global Future*,[3] the NIC focuses on three relative certainties: 1) the irreversibility and growth of the 'mega-trend' of globalisation with the spread of global firms and technologies; 2) The greatest benefits of globalisation will accrue to countries and groups that can access and adopt new technologies; 3) Multinationals will be outside the control of any one state and will be key agents of change through widely dispersing technology. Uncertainty stems from the fact that the benefits of globalisation will not be universal, and conflicts, instability, environmental and ethical issues will rise to the fore even more, with non-Western players setting new 'rules of the game'. In contrast, Mike Davis paints a starker picture, where the Reagan/Thatcher financial deregulation during the 1980s created a 'Planet of Slums'. Davis argues that strategies of 'individual responsibility' and little state involvement, in place of the old government Welfare State subsidy system, unleashed the century's massive wave of uncontrolled, informal urbanisation.

This issue correlates these two interpretations and characterises the emerging 21st-century global city through shifting relationships between four emerging models:

Model 1

The 21st-century city is managed through nodes of high-density *technopoles*. Corporate enclaves house high-end offices, exclusive condominiums and entertainment centres. These nodes occupy zones in older city centres, high-technology clusters called edge cities, resort and recreational spots around the world, and high-density hubs such as airports, theme parks or megamalls. In 2004, London's Heathrow Airport handled 64 million people, Disneyworld hosted 36 million, while the Mall of America entertained 46 million visitors. Several malls much larger than the Mall of America have recently opened in China, with more even larger ones soon to appear.

Model 2

The self-organised *informal city* constitutes the majority of current global urbanisation, and is the antipode of the technopoles. This is a world of self-built homes for a new urban proletariat in megacity regions with populations that are estimated to be as high as 30 million in Lagos and 19 million in Mexico City. In addition to the informal settlements that ring developing cities, refugees, illegal immigrants and the grey economy labour under cover servicing the global technopoles.

Model 3

Global *conurbations* comprise semiregulated capitalist developments populated with seminomadic professional 're-los'. This is a hierarchical system with a few global financial and political centres directing a chain of command through vast intercity regions. Megacities like the US Northeast Megalopolis, Los Angeles–San Diego, San Francisco–Oakland–Silicon Valley, the Tokyo–Yokohama –Osaka corridor, the Rhine and Pearl River deltas already contain over half the world's population.

Model 4

The remotely monitored and managed *forest and agribusiness machine* nourishes and feeds these vast urban agglomerations with a tiny labour force. Such areas include abandoned and fallow forest and farmland used also for the protection of water supplies and for recreational purposes, but they are continually encroached upon by extensive re-lo sprawl.

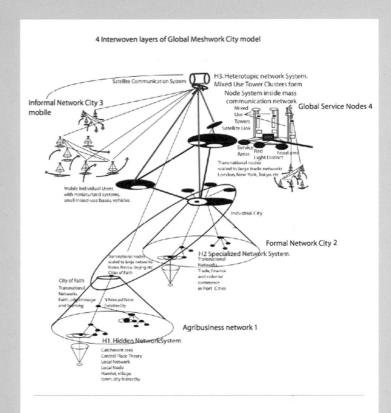

Compression and dispersal in the meshwork city. Four overlapping models operate in different combinations to form the emerging, highly differentiated patchworks, linked together to create a new global city. Compressed layers of networks flattened in the meshwork city can all be present in a particular city simultaneously, represented as a series of patches containing different systems of organisation, depending on the dominant power of particular urban actors in each patch, city, network or mesh.

The current promise and potential for design is to combine remote sensing with hand-held devices to monitor, measure and redirect patches of deregulated urban growth through telecommunications-enhanced local feedback loops. Can vast settlement patterns be precisely calibrated over time with local managers mitigating environmental impacts? Will a wide-access network help allocate resources and redirect aid more locally and equitably? From the remote platform, city and nature are an intricate mix. Human settlements are just one element in a complex, global ecosystem where land-cover patches are remotely classified by building type, spectral mix, temperature variation, reflectivity, surface permeability and vegetation patterns, creating unique city signatures constantly reshaped by local actors. The spectre of a panoptic dimension of state-controlled remote technology can be turned to the practical synoptic possibility of multiple civic eyes on the planet, on cities, and on government and big business. Local actors can seek a global overview from multiple platforms, which can theoretically replace top-down, bureaucratic urban surveying systems.

Korean Cyber-Bangs: Seoul

A couple are watching a movie on a state-of-the-art home theatre system within a small room in a four-storey walk-up building. A group of students are singing karaoke songs in the basement and, across the street, a group is meeting to work on a term paper, on computers rented by the hour. Around them, schoolboys are gaming and video chatting. They could not do this in their families' homes. Outside, glowing signs announce that similar activities are taking place in *bangs* (rooms) all along the busy street.

Modern bangs provide privacy and technological services for work and play in small spaces available for the public to rent out for short periods of time, measured in minutes or by the length of a movie. They are a natural consequence of a society congested in space and time. There are different types of bangs. Norebangs are karaoke rooms, PC bangs are cybercafés, and DVD bangs are for viewing rented movies. Traditionally, dabangs (tearooms) were places for literary discussion and production.

High-density bang areas are typically found around major universities and large schools. Their early appearance and success facilitated the development of Internet infrastructure in Seoul[1] by creating economic pools of use. South Korea is at the forefront of Internet and wireless communications technology and use.

Bangs are a versatile typology that fits in small spaces, basements and upper floors, surrounded by different uses such as retail, office or housing. Providing a sense of temporary community, they make use of less desirable floor space, extending and transforming the life and use of buildings that may not otherwise be profitable to owners. Many also create 24-hour flows of people, improving the sense of community, liveliness and safety – transforming the city from within.

Note
1 B Park and T Gillespie, 'PC Bang Brought a Big Bang: The Unique Aspect of the Korean Internet Industry', *The Journal of Education, Community, and Values* 3(8), 2003.

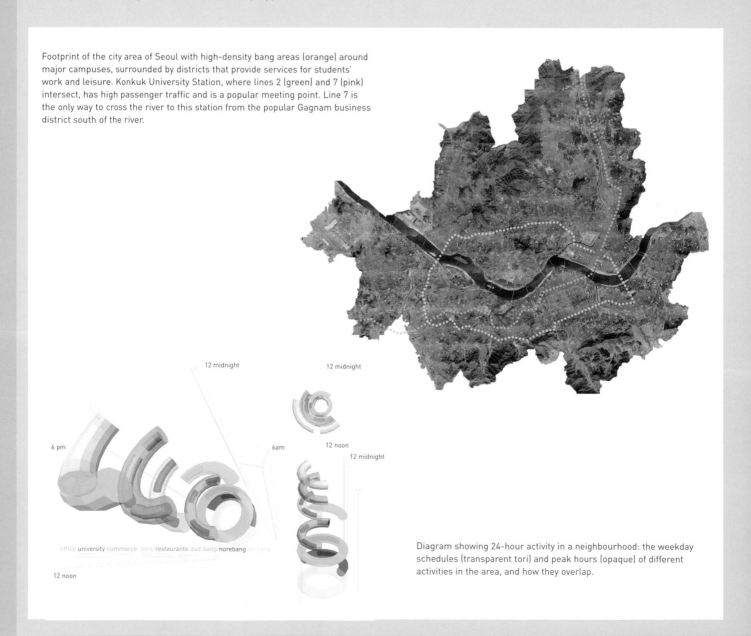

Footprint of the city area of Seoul with high-density bang areas (orange) around major campuses, surrounded by districts that provide services for students' work and leisure. Konkuk University Station, where lines 2 (green) and 7 (pink) intersect, has high passenger traffic and is a popular meeting point. Line 7 is the only way to cross the river to this station from the popular Gagnam business district south of the river.

Diagram showing 24-hour activity in a neighbourhood: the weekday schedules (transparent tori) and peak hours (opaque) of different activities in the area, and how they overlap.

Street corner outside the Konkuk University sky-train station, a popular place for young people to meet.

The penetration of high-tech bangs and shop fronts into low-rise, formerly residential areas creates the contrast of busy, lit commercial and entertainment street front and dark entrances to alleys of apartments and houses.

Streetscape of bangs. This area of buildings of between four and five storeys high has seen its interior spaces filled with various leisure facilities: restaurants, bars, norebangs (karaoke), DVD and PC bangs are plentiful. There are also spaces for rent in which groups of friends can play board games, just as people would do in their homes in the West.

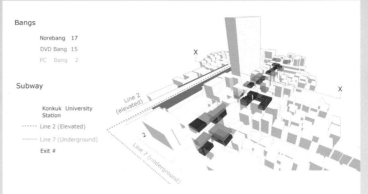

Bangs

    Norebang 17
    DVD Bang 15
    PC Bang   2

Subway

    Konkuk University
    Station
----- Line 2 (Elevated)
----- Line 7 (Underground)
    Exit #

3-D mapping of bangs along a street in the Hwayang-Dong area. The bangs tend to be on upper floors or in basements, indicating that lower-rent spaces are good enough for such purposes. Exit 2 of the train station reconciles the flow from the underground and elevated lines.

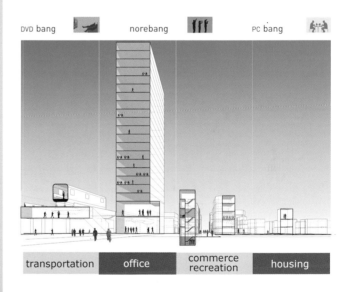

DVD bang   norebang   PC bang

| transportation | office | commerce recreation | housing |

Section X-X showing a slice through the neighbourhood programmes, revealing bangs in upper floors and basements.

Clockwise from top left: Corridor with many doors; interior of DVD bang viewing booth; interior of norebang (karaoke); interior of PC bang.

Grounding Remote Sensing: Pixels, Polygons, Patches and People

A startling new image of our urbanised planet appeared at the end of the 20th century: the composite nighttime-light satellite image tiled from data gathered by the US National Oceanic and Atmospheric Agency (NOAA). The agency's Nighttime Lights of the World map stunningly depicts the overall shape of the emerging 21st-century city – both its conurbations and its road networks. Civil remote sensing has been available since 1972, and Landsat 1 through 7[4] offers a continuous 30-year multispectral record of the formation of the century's global city. But images from satellites are limited by the coarseness of their grain; for example, at 30 metres to a pixel, Landsat works for regional land-cover studies, but is useless at building scale. However, new satellites such as IKONOS and Quick Bird capture up to sub-metre resolution, while nonorbital aerial platforms offer even sharper images. The US military's Urban Tactical Planner combines high-resolution imagery and computer software to manoeuvre in maze-like cities. During the Iraq War, spy drones over Falluja captured detailed 3-D

images block by block in real time. And Google Earth allows web users to similarly zoom in to a 3-D image of any city.

Civilian uses of remote sensing and hand-held devices will redefine the 21st-century city – not only its limits and patterns, but also its modes of sociopolitical interaction. Satellites provide wide spectral information based on sunlight reflectance that are read by trained observers on computers. The basic skills were derived from aerial reconnaissance during the Second World War for targeting purposes. Pioneering ecologists are developing pattern-recognition techniques as ways of recognising variations of human activity as differentiated landscape mosaics with reflective textures, patches, places of change (turbulence) and settled patterns (repose). Ecosystem science grew out of observing biological interactions in bounded areas such as small watersheds or islands through time cycles of disturbance and resilience. The Human Ecosystem Framework and Patch Dynamic theory models interactions between actors and flows within bounded territories, mixing in particular patterns. Ecologists, through close-up field research, explain how patches maintained their identity through mutuality, redundancy and tight feedback loops that reinforced self-organising patterns in local networks of complex adaptive systems.

Crucial to recognising these self-organising processes as patterns in space and time is the frequent passage of satellites, providing snapshots at intervals showing, for example, the various courses taken by a fire or flood, the shifting of urban and forest edges, the expansion and shrinking of agricultural lands, or the abandonment and decay of rustbelt inner-city neighbourhoods. As part of the Baltimore Ecosystem Study (BES), scientists, designers and community organisations are working together using remote sensing and close-up observation to develop automated pattern recognition – to classify biophysical and social patches, and change detection – to model how different patches grow or shrink over time. Computer programs scanning satellite imagery can look for traces of specific activities or settlement patterns. The array of reflective patterns that can be recognised, and their urban correlates, has expanded so that scientists and designers are hoping to train computers to scan urban formations to look for settlement patterns from different periods, created under different regulatory regimes in cities' histories, with different registers of building, landscaping, water management and biomass.

Climate change or natural disaster scenarios combine close-up and remote sensing by constructing models of cities and their probable vulnerabilities together with robotic localised monitoring. The pre-eminent hubs of the emerging global network city are all extremely vulnerable to the impacts of global warming as icebergs melt and seas rise. Both London and Tokyo, built close to sea level, are preparing their defences, unlike the cities of the US east coast. In such hyperdense global nodes, remote sensing, GIS, satellites, GPS, wireless, broadband and the Internet combine to create new forms of design practice engaged with a wide range of agents and actors where city topography dominates the discourse of the potential for remote and close-up sensing.

USGS
2000
Level 2

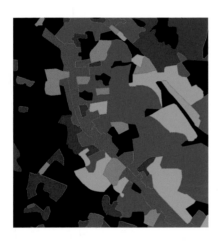

HERCULES

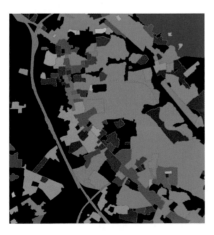

Two classifications of the same 18-square-kilometre area in Baltimore County, Maryland, US. The top panel displays standard land-use categories from the classification derived by Anderson in 1976.[5] The bottom panel displays the land-cover classification Cadenasso and Pickett referred to as HERCULES. In both panels, only land area that contains built structures is shown in colour. Land cover with no built structures is masked in black. Note the finer categorical and spatial resolution obtained by using the HERCULES classification, which focuses on land cover as opposed to land use, and incorporates both built structures and associated vegetation characteristics into class definitions.

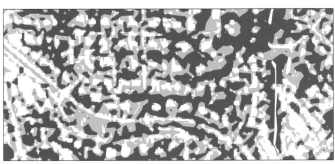

KEY

 Block Groups

 Vegetation

Per cent Vegetation

Less

More

 Property Parcels

Vegetation

 Grass

Trees

Comparison of (left) relatively coarse-scale (1:100,000) and (right) fine-scale (1:10,000) vegetation analysis that can be performed using Landsat-derived vegetation data and Census Block Groups, and IKONOS-derived vegetation data and property parcels. Remote sensing and census data is combined in this overlay system in order to relate vegetation and social patterns.

Million-Dollar Blocks: Wichita, Kansas

'Million-Dollar Blocks' describes the result of visualising traditional criminal-justice data with new geographic tools. Million-Dollar Blocks are single-census blocks in inner-city neighbourhoods for which over a million dollars are spent each year to imprison residents from those blocks.

Although incarceration decisions are made individually, one person at a time, when mapped collectively over the course of a year the data reveal patterns, presence and gaps previously hidden from traditional examination. The maps present a new way of understanding the opportunity costs of mass incarceration, concentrating on the residents of particular neighbourhoods. Measured in dollars, and compared against other government expenditure, the data reveals that the prison system is the most

important government institution in such neighbourhoods.

Maps and datasets are never neutral, and these are no exception. The datasets existed. They were produced to make a record of people entering the criminal-justice system. Million-Dollar Blocks mapping uses the data another way – to highlight a trade-off. By privileging the home address, neighbourhood and community of the incarcerated individual, prison expenditure maps turn traditional maps of disadvantage into maps of investment opportunity. The resulting pictures direct focus: the seemingly predictable census blocks in which people in the database have lived, and to which they will return. Once the home address is privileged, architecture is on trial.

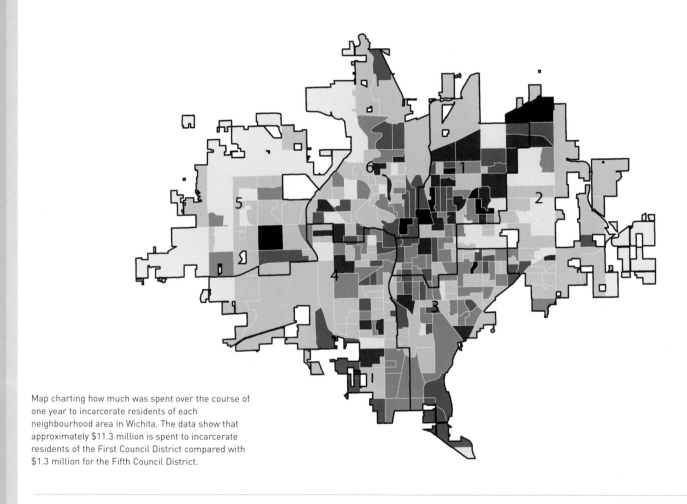

Map charting how much was spent over the course of one year to incarcerate residents of each neighbourhood area in Wichita. The data show that approximately $11.3 million is spent to incarcerate residents of the First Council District compared with $1.3 million for the Fifth Council District.

Map demonstrating that for each district, the vast majority of the people sent to prison, and therefore those representing the greatest expenditure, are individuals who were returned, for short periods of time, for violating conditions of parole.

	NEW COMMITMENT	PROBATION REVOCATION	PAROLE REVOCATION
DISTRICT 1 ($11,389,702)	$5.8	$2.5	$3.1
DISTRICT 2 ($2,026,126)	$0.9	$0.7	$0.4
DISTRICT 3 ($4,933,039)	$2.3	$1.0	$1.2
DISTRICT 4 ($4,157,792)	$1.9	$0.9	$1.3
DISTRICT 5 ($1,379,792)	$0.7	$0.09	$0.5
DISTRICT 6 ($5,038,944)	$1.8	$1.2	$1.2

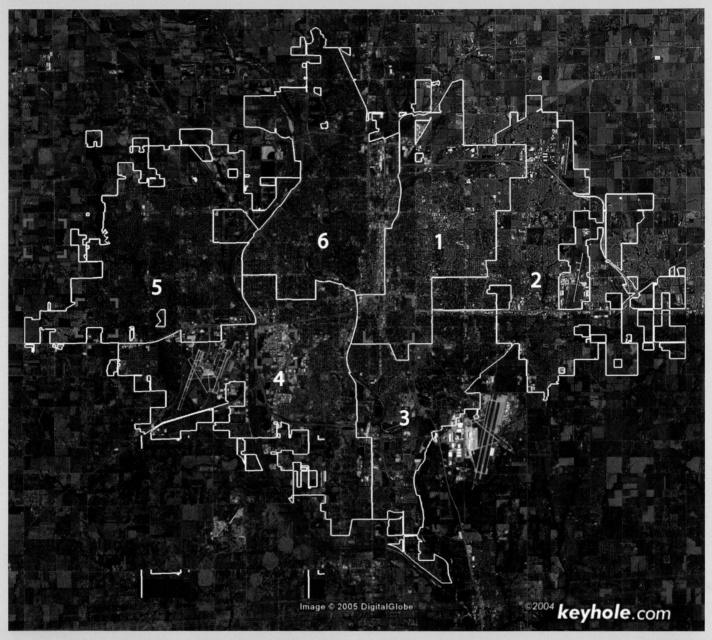

6
1
5
2
4
3

Image © 2005 DigitalGlobe

©2004 *keyhole*.com

Images captured from Keyhole (www.keyhole.com) with district council boundaries overlaid onto satellite imagery. Kansas is a Midwestern city in the US with a population of roughly 360,000. Visible here is a city surrounded by farmlands laid out on the one-mile grid that organises a large part of the US landscape. Panning across Wichita with a more detailed zoom reveals other familiar contemporary organisations typical of this kind of US city: moving inwards from the farmlands are gated communities, industrial zones and, finally, the inner city.

This project is the first collaboration between the Justice Mapping Center (directed by Eric Cadora) and the Spatial Information Design Lab (SIDL) (directed by Laura Kurgan), at the Graduate School of Architecture Planning and Preservation (GSAPP), Columbia University. The project, 'Graphical Innovations in Justice Mapping', will continue to work in selected states in the US. It has been funded by the Open Society Institute, JEHT Foundation.
Project Team: Teresa Ball, David Reinfurt, Seth Spielman and Charles Swartz.

Map of areas covered in this issue
The introduction and first section of the issue travel the globe searching out close-up and remote observations of the 21st-century city. The last three sections focus on three regional arenas: Western Europe, South Asia and North America.

Sensing the City: New Forms of Practice

The human senses – eyes, ears, noses, hands and feet – on the ground are crucial to testing the hypotheses of remote global monitors. Terrestrial observers usually develop alternative theses based on direct observation. The 20th century witnessed a vast move to urban agglomerations on a scale before unknown. Fossil fuels powered and enhanced global mass movements, enriching and empowering a handful of players. We are now realising the enormous social and environmental costs of this pattern of development: huge expenses for air, ground and water remediation, global warming, corruption and vast economic inequalities. The great opportunity of the 21st-century city is for both close-up and remote modes of observation to be linked in a system of two-way feedback loops that allows a collaborative picture of local and global environments.

The dual challenges to end poverty and repair damaged environments are basic to the UN's 21st Century Millennium Ecosystem Assessment and Millennium Development Goals. In these plans, remote-sensing-based global mapping projects are combined with small-scale recommendations to fast-track aid for the next 10 years, scaling up public investments with 'quick wins' such as mass distribution of malaria nets, removing fees for primary education and essential health services, expansion of school-meals programmes to cover children in hunger hot spots, and massive replenishment of soil nutrients for subsistence farmers. Strategically assisted micro-improvements contribute to regional economic growth. Hand-held devices will be essential for these programmes that tie together remote understanding of the ecosystem with local needs and services as drivers of bottom-up change.

The Center for International Earth Science Information Network (CIESIN) at Columbia University is developing tools such as the Global Rural Urban Mapping Program using the NOAA's nighttime light data, Landsat and local tabular information to more accurately spatialise urban population projections as a dynamic series of patches, including health and socioeconomic indicators. According to demographer Deborah Balk, child mortality in Africa increases with distance from a city of 50,000. CIESIN's mapping efforts give a much more accurate picture of where people are moving now, and will assist in locating infrastructure, health clinics and schools. Cellular granulation and flow in the informal, self-built additions to emerging cities is obvious, as settlers first build small, isolated structures that expand either horizontally or vertically to form a carpet or matrix of housing. Migration flows result in extraordinarily high densities and very complex, 3-D spatial configurations. Through remote sensing and close-up observation, informal network cities can be identified as distinct urban patchworks with their own dynamics, forming a base for research assessing and monitoring ecosystem change and human migration patterns through a multiscaled approach.

The urban granulation of a typical informal housing settlement has its formal equivalent in the developed world's picturesque, sprawling, car-based suburban model. In the BES, for example, remote sensing and close-up field surveys monitor shifting relationships between patches of forest, agriculture, watershed and human settlement patterns as part of long-term ecological research. Columbia University's Urban Design Studio developed a watershed urban ecosystem approach in the early 2000s, in collaboration with the BES scientists. This model, employed in shrinking older postindustrial cities, can also be tested in fringe urbanisation or rapidly growing informal settlements. The Baltimore watershed approach stretches from inner-city neighbourhoods to the agricultural and forest fringe, crossing previous political and urban/rural classification divisions towards a patch dynamics approach that looks at coupling human and environmental systems in locally based feedback loops.

The study of urban form in time, morphogenesis could provide flexible and resilient designs for vulnerable sites within unpredictable scenarios. Morphogenetic studies

Ecosystem monitoring systems developed in the Hubbard Brook experimental forest in New Hampshire are tested in West Baltimore by urban design students at Columbia University's Graduate School of Architecture Planning and Preservation. The goal is to create block-specific neighbourhood development plans based on storm-water management and gardening.

make a basic distinction between flow and stasis in the city. Remote and close-up observations monitor speed and eddies, mapping self-organisational patterns and networks of relationships in differentiated channels of flow. Currents amplify small differences in speed and direction of flow to form eddies and feedback loops, allowing the emergence of cellular islands and patches with different textures. These granulated textures are the result of the coagulation of isolated objects trapped in the flow.

While this description was written with the flows of a river in mind, it applies equally well as a metaphor for vehicular traffic flowing along highways, trains on railway tracks or ships in docks and harbours, pedestrians in a large city, distribution networks, waste streams, or information on global networks. Such are the possibilities and potential of the flattened 21st-century global meshwork city, with local actors slightly adjusting the global environment through networks of collaboration and cooperation. ∆

Notes
1 Janet Abu-Lughod, *Before European Hegemony: The World System AD 1250–1350*, Oxford University Press (Oxford), 1989.
2 Peter Taylor, *World City Network: A Global Urban Analysis*, Routledge (London), 2003.
3 www.cia.gov.nic/NIC.globaltrend2020.html.
4 US satellites have together provided the longest continuous record of earth's land surfaces and coastal areas by capturing surface reflectance data within a wide spectral range.
5 James R Anderson et al, *A Land Use and Land Classification System for use with Remote Sensing Data*, Government Printing Office (Washington DC), 1976.

The authors would like to thank Roberta Balstad and Deborah Balk from the Center for International Earth Science Information Network, Christopher Small from Lamont Doherty Earth Observatory, Steward Pickett from the Institute of Ecosystem Studies, Mary Cadenasso from Yale School of Forestry and Environmental Studies, Morgan Grove from the US Forest Service Northeast Research Station, as well as Austin Troy and Jarlath O'Neil-Dunne from the University of Vermont School of Natural Resources Spatial Information Lab for kindly allowing us to interview them for this essay.

Intense Multiplicity: Bangkok

Bangkok's attempt to solve its ultimate riddle – its traffic congestion – resulted in the outrageous solution of inserting a monstrous mass transit system into the already dense, if not chaotic, urban fabric. Built through the painful period of economic collapse, the new elevated train system – the BTS SkyTrain – became operational in 1999.

Six years on, it has attained a unique status as the icon of contemporary Bangkok. Its overwhelming presence is featured in every conceivable media – new music videos, movies or advertisements. The SkyTrain is an indispensable symbol of the new generation. Its new mode of movement, floating high above the ground, allows the commercial buildings that exist along its 13-kilometre distance to 'plug-in' to their nearest stations, sucking on commuters to engage in shopping activities, forming a new type of hypershopping experience – a central shopping district. The SkyTrain functions as an organ of capital flow.

In 2004 came the BTS SkyTrain's alter ego: the underground line – the MRT Subway. Submerged and invisible, its presence (or lack of it) may not achieve the status quo of the SkyTrain, yet curious transformations are manifesting themselves in the vicinity where the two systems intersect.

The configurations of the BTS–MRT interchanges (Jatujak, Silom and Asok) emerged from the way the stations, and their connections, are located and how they adapt to the physicality of each area by squeezing themselves into and spreading across the richly textured fabric. At the Silom and Asok interchanges, such configurations generate a hybrid movement where commuters are mechanically catapulted between stations, seamlessly flowing between their multiple levels and threading diverse programmes – food vendors, flea markets, convenience stores, fitness centres, shopping malls and motorcycle taxis – into a continuum. With such movement, engagement with activities turns into a single fluid motion, condensed into close proximities and consumed within a matter of minutes. Bangkok's excessiveness is even more exposed. The interchange is the apparatus that reveals a new-found path of intense multiplicity.

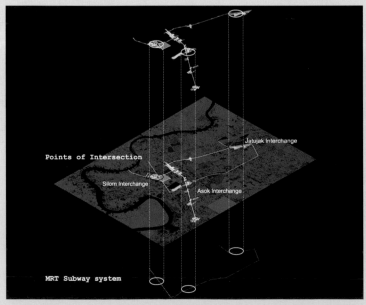

Map of Bangkok's two mass transit systems.

Multiple levels of movement around the intersection.

The daunting megastructure of the BTS Skytrain.

The 'skywalk' feeding commuters to the shopping complex.

View from the Asok's metro station entrance across the road, looking towards the SkyTrain station and interchange.

Engagement with diverse activities.

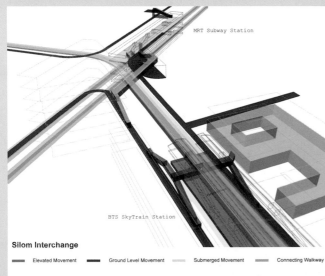

MRT Subway Station

BTS SkyTrain Station

Silom Interchange

—— Elevated Movement   —— Ground Level Movement   —— Submerged Movement   —— Connecting Walkway

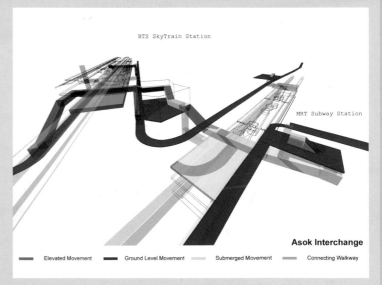

BTS SkyTrain Station

MRT Subway Station

Asok Interchange

—— Elevated Movement   —— Ground Level Movement   —— Submerged Movement   —— Connecting Walkway

Configuration of the Silom interchange showing the station and the connections that stretch out over (and under) the city fabric.

Asok interchange illustrating the path of hybrid movement, but with different configurations.

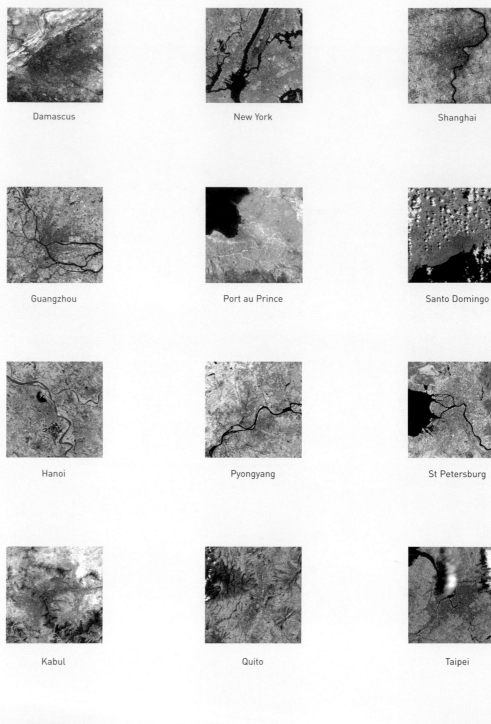

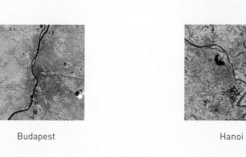

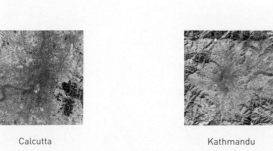

Bangalore

Damascus

New York

Shanghai

Beirut

Guangzhou

Port au Prince

Santo Domingo

Budapest

Hanoi

Pyongyang

St Petersburg

Cairo

Kabul

Quito

Taipei

Calcutta

Kathmandu

San Salvador

Tianjin

Cities from space
Visible/infrared images collected by Landsat 7 in 1999 and 2000. Each image represents 30 x 30 square kilometres. Colours correspond to visible and infrared brightness at specific wavelengths. A full-resolution gallery of these and other cities is available online at www.LDEO.columbia.edu/~small/Urban.html.

Calgary

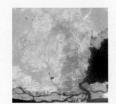

Lagos

São Paulo

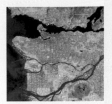

Vancouver

URBAN REMOTE SENSING:
GLOBAL COMPARISONS

Over three decades of satellite remote sensing has supplied a rich, largely untapped archive for urban designers and thinkers. Existing and concurrent images have the potential to allow us not only to trace through multitemporal observations of urban agglomerations, but also to predict emerging urban trends. **Christopher Small** of the Lamont-Doherty Earth Observatory of Columbia University provides some essential insights into the applications of remote-sensing technology, while also outlining its capabilities and limitations.

Chicago

Miami

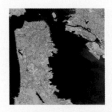

San Francisco

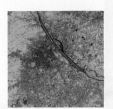

Vienna

Remotely sensed observations of cities and their hinterlands provide unique perspectives on the diversity of urban environments over a wide range of spatial and temporal scales. Optical, thermal and microwave radar sensors reveal characteristics of the urban environment not visible to the unaided eye. The instantaneous panoramic, or synoptic, perspective of the satellite (or aircraft) combined with the broadband sensitivity of these sensors provides a wealth of information about the urban environment that often cannot be obtained from ground-level observations. Examples range from mapping informal settlements to monitoring the health of urban vegetation, to modelling regional-scale climate dynamics. Recently launched high-resolution sensors, like *Quickbird* and

IKONOS, combined with 30-year archives of moderate-resolution Landsat and SPOT imagery, now provide detailed multitemporal observations of every city on earth.

The three primary applications of remote sensing are mapping, monitoring and modelling. The use of remote sensing in mapping is the most obvious, as imaging sensors collect and render information in the inherently spatial form of a map. The precise control and geometric registration of modern imaging systems allows the geographic location of an individual image pixel to be determined to within metres from sensor altitudes of hundreds of kilometres. The perspective offered by sensors on satellites provides instantaneous snapshots of large areas at regular time intervals, thereby providing a more spatially complete representation of the earth's surface than could reasonably be obtained from ground-based measurements. The geometric precision of the images combined with repeated revisits provided by a satellite orbit extends spatial mapping into the time dimension and makes it possible to monitor subtle changes in the earth's surface.

Quantifying spatial and temporal changes in the physical properties (for example, colour, temperature, surface texture) of the earth's surface provides a dynamic representation of the anthropogenic, climatic, hydrological and ecological processes affecting our environment. This makes it possible for scientists to develop mathematical models of these processes and, in some cases, predict their behaviour. Accurate and detailed observations are essential for the models to have such predictive power. A familiar example of physical modelling is weather prediction. The mathematical models that provide our weather forecasts rely heavily on inputs from remotely sensed observations.

Insights gained from the study of remotely sensed observations provide the understanding necessary to devise and refine these models. In fact, changes in land cover are now believed to have at least as strong an influence on climate as greenhouse gases. Land-cover configurations in and around urban areas also influence regional climate. Advances in our understanding of other dynamic processes now facilitate development of further models to predict the behaviour of ground water and contaminants, air pollution, endemic and invasive species, and even human activities such as urban growth and sprawl. Remotely sensed measurements are essential to all of these.

Recent comparative studies of urban areas and their surrounding hinterlands reveal both consistencies and differences among a variety of cities. The fundamental characteristic of cities that emerges is their heterogeneity. More so than any other type of land cover, cities are heterogeneous mosaics of an enormous variety of different types of surfaces at a range of different scales. Heterogeneity of urban form and function is manifested as heterogeneity of reflectance. Reflectance is the physical characteristic of an object that determines what we perceive as colour. While this diversity and multiscale heterogeneity has confounded past attempts to classify and characterise urban systems with satellite imagery, it now provides a way to quantify these systems. The standard approach to classifying land cover is based on homogeneity and consistency of reflectance. Urban land cover, however, may be more effectively distinguished on the basis of its heterogeneity relative to other types of land cover (for example, forest, agriculture, desert soil).

By their nature, cities are heterogeneous agglomerates of organisms, materials and energy that do not otherwise occur in nature. In the illustrated collection of satellite images for 28 cities around the world, each image is a 'false colour' composite, where the colours correspond to both visible and infrared reflectance. The variability of spatial form and reflectance of these images is the cumulative result of a succession of physical,

historical, cultural, political and socioeconomic processes for each of the cities. However, there are also physical consistencies across all of the images that allow us to understand processes operative in these cities and their hinterlands.

Resolution

To make use of the information contained in remotely sensed images it is necessary to understand what the images represent and what their limitations are. Specifically, we need to understand what the sensors can detect and what they cannot. The capabilities and limitations of remote sensing are dictated by the spatial, spectral and temporal resolution of the observations. Spatial resolution determines both how large and how small an object can be imaged. Spectral resolution determines how many and which colours (both visible and infrared) can be distinguished. Temporal resolution determines how frequently the surface is imaged through time as satellites pass overhead.

Many aspects of optical remote sensing can be understood by analogy to simple digital cameras. Multispectral sensors are conceptually similar to digital cameras in that both collect and render images of the brightness of reflected light. In both cases, white light from the sun illuminates a surface, and some fraction of the incident light is reflected from the surface back into the sensor to render a brightness image. The colour of each ray of reflected light is determined by the physical properties of the surface it is reflected from. Just as digital cameras record the intensity of visible red, green and blue light as three complementary brightness images, multispectral sensors measure the intensity of both visible and infrared light as a larger number of brightness images corresponding to specific wavelengths (colours) of light. Aside from cost, the primary difference between a digital camera and a multispectral sensor is that most multispectral sensors are sensitive to several different wavelengths of visible and infrared light.

Every optical sensor has trade-off limited spatial and spectral resolution. This means that sensors that image more colours must have lower spatial resolution (larger pixels), while sensors that image only total brightness (analogous to black-and-white images) can resolve smaller pixels (all else being equal). The hunger for

New York City multiresolution trade-offs
Satellite views of Upper Manhattan at different spatial and spectral resolutions. Archives of moderate-resolution Landsat imagery resolve seasonal to interannual changes in visible/infrared reflectance over the past 30 years. High-resolution IKONOS imagery provides metre-scale resolution showing the individual components of the urban mosaic. (Includes materials © Space Imaging)

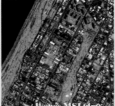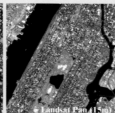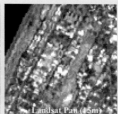

Landsat ETM (30m)   Landsat ETM (30m)   Ikonos MSI (4m)   Landsat Pan (15m)   Landsat Pan (15m)   Ikonos Pan (1m)

Spectral mixing space of a digital photograph

Three orthogonal views of the spectral mixing space for a digital photograph of a New York City street scene. Each pixel in the photograph corresponds to a point in a 3-D cloud of pixels defining the spectral mixing space. The 3-D cloud is shown from three orthogonal perspectives, and the colour of the cloud indicates the density of pixels in that part of the cloud. Warmer colours correspond to greater numbers of pixels. The red, green and blue brightnesses of each pixel determines its location within the cloud.

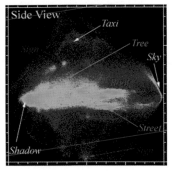

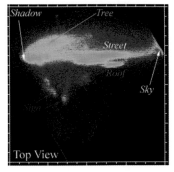

spectral resolution comes from our desire to image as many different spectral wavelength bands as possible to distinguish more distinct colours – both visible and infrared. A comparison of Landsat and IKONOS imagery provides an example of these trade-offs with images of Manhattan. While the Landsat sensor provides greater spectral resolution by imaging more spectral bands (6 vs 4 wavelengths), the IKONOS sensor provides greater spatial resolution by imaging smaller pixels (4 vs 30 metres). Both sensors also illustrate the trade-off individually by collecting both lower spatial resolution multispectral (colour) and higher spatial resolution panchromatic (grey) images. Similarly, the limited storage and communications bandwidth of modern satellites means that sensors that image smaller pixels must also image narrower ground-swathes. Thus, the increase in spatial resolution generally comes at the expense of the sensor's ground-swathe width or image area as well as the number of wavelength bands.

Spatial Resolution and Spectral Mixing

The limited spatial resolution of any sensor leads to the process of spectral mixing within each pixel. In the case of Landsat, this means that the colour of each pixel is the average of the colours of all the illuminated surfaces within the pixel's 30 x 30-square-metre footprint on the ground. The fact that very few areas within the urban mosaic are homogeneous at 30-metre scales means that almost all urban areas imaged by Landsat are imaged as mixed pixels. While this fact has confounded attempts to classify urban land cover on the basis of unique colours, it does provide a way to represent the physical properties of urban areas as mixtures of spectrally distinct biophysical land covers (for example, vegetation, soil, asphalt, cement and water) known as endmembers. This is important because it makes it possible to mathematically 'unmix' each pixel to produce physically based abundance maps of each land-cover type – even when the actual features corresponding to the spectral endmembers are smaller than the pixel size. For example, the Landsat sensor can detect the presence of a tree within a single pixel, despite the fact that the tree is much smaller than the area of the pixel. By mapping spatial variations in the fractional abundance of different endmembers, we can map spatial variations in landscape characteristics such as vegetation density, soil type and water colour. Knowledge of these different percentages of reflectance is necessary to build the process models described above, and has intrinsic importance to a wide range of mapping and monitoring applications.

An alternative conceptual framework for understanding multispectral images, known as a mixing space, allows us to represent images as varying mixtures of specific biophysical landscape components such as vegetation, soil, asphalt and water. The concept of the mixing space is analogous to a colour space and is valuable because it provides a representation where pixels of similar colour cluster together, distinct from other clusters of pixels with different colours. This makes it possible to isolate all pixels of a given colour (hence physical property) by their proximity in the mixing space – regardless of the complexity of their spatial distribution in the corresponding geographic space. This is possible because these components correspond to the distinct spectral endmembers referred to above. In addition to the familiar spatial/geographic coordinate system provided by a colour or multispectral image, there exists a complementary colour

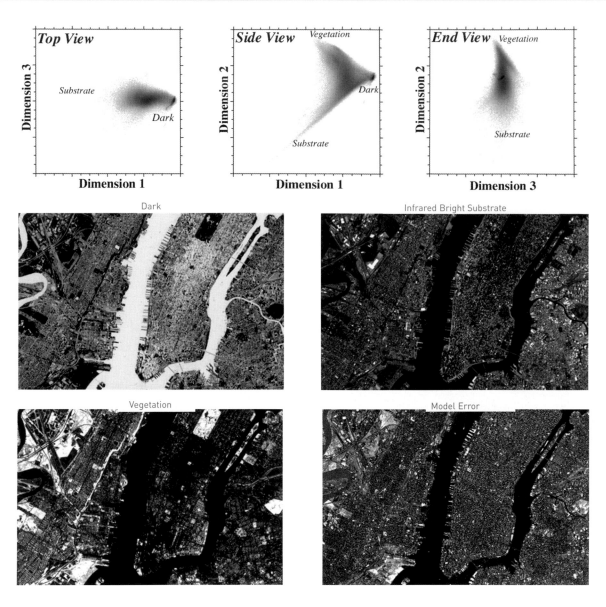

New York City mixing space and endmembers
Analogous to the preceding figure, each pixel in the six-layer multispectral satellite image corresponds to a point in a 6-D visible/infrared spectral mixing space. Orthogonal perspectives of the three primary dimensions of the 6-D cloud are shown above abundance maps for the three spectral endmembers at the apexes of the pixel cloud. Lighter areas on the maps correspond to greater abundances of infrared-bright Substrate, Vegetation and nonreflective Dark surface. Lighter areas on the error image (lower right) show land-cover types for which the three-endmember mixture model is less accurate.

space in which each pixel occupies a distinct location determined by its colour. Representing the colour of each pixel in a digital image with its corresponding red, green and blue (RGB) values allows the pixels in any image to be represented as a point cloud in a 3-D colour space of red, green and blue brightness.

Since most pixels in most images are not purely red, green or blue (but rather mixtures of red, green and blue) the familiar RGB colour space can be thought of as a visible mixing space. In the duality of geographic and spectral spaces, each distinct colour becomes equivalent to a unique location in the spectral mixing space. The idea can be extended to multispectral images by adding infrared dimensions to the colour/mixing space. This is important because it allows us to map land-surface types on the basis of colour similarity regardless of how complex their spatial distributions.

Spectral Resolution and Hyperspectral Remote Sensing
The current state-of-the-art in optical remote sensing involves hyperspectral airborne sensors with very high spectral resolution. These hyperspectral sensors can detect narrow, wavelength-specific patterns related to the molecular absorption of light in specific types of materials. Some examples of these absorption features are illustrated in the reflectance spectra and hyperspectral image cube opposite. The subtle differences in colour (visible and infrared) that can be resolved in these hyperdimensional mixing spaces make it possible to discriminate between materials that would be indistinguishable at visible wavelengths. While hyperspectral sensors provide an essentially continuous reflectance spectrum for each pixel in the image, broadband

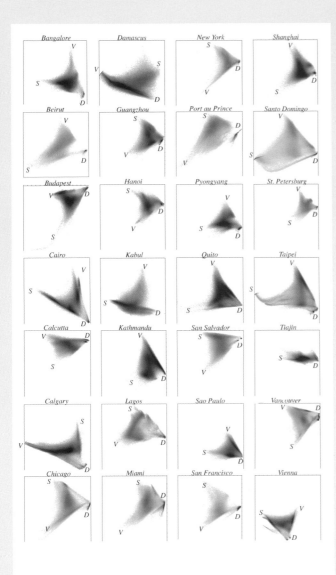

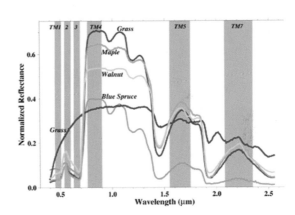

Urban spectral mixing spaces
Density-shaded mixing spaces for the 28 diverse cities shown previously. The triangular shape and consistent spectral endmembers at the apexes are significant. Endmembers S, V and D correspond to infrared-bright Substrate, Vegetation and nonreflexive Dark surface. The orientation of the triangular mixing spaces is arbitrary.

Hyperspectral cube and laboratory spectra
Hyperspectral cube collected by the AVIRIS sensor, built and operated by NASA's Jet Propulsion Laboratory. Each pixel in the cube corresponds to a full spectrum like those shown on the plot. Warmer colours on the sides of the cube correspond to higher reflectances at that wavelength. Subtle differences in the shape of the spectra distinguish different types of vegetation and soil.

sensors (like Landsat, IKONOS and digital cameras) image only a few broad bands of wavelengths and cannot resolve these narrow absorptions. When hyperspectral images are analysed using mixing spaces, it is possible to distinguish a much wider variety of subtle colour variations because the aforementioned clustering occurs in a mixing space with tens or hundreds of dimensions. Hyperspectral imagery is currently being used to map deposits of economically valuable minerals and to monitor the health of vegetation in agriculture and silviculture

Implications
The potential applications of remote sensing for earth observation are largely untapped. Archives of imagery from a variety of satellite sensors provide a 30-year record of changes in the earth's surface. Much of the growth and evolution of the world's cities has occurred in this time. Urban growth is manifest at spatial scales of kilometres and temporal scales of years, thus these archives of moderate-resolution imagery provide an opportunity to quantify and perhaps model urban evolution at spatial and temporal scales where direct human observation is otherwise difficult or impossible.

Global coverage allows comparative analyses of large numbers of cities in different settings so that consistent patterns might be detected among urban systems in diverse environmental, cultural and socioeconomic contexts. Recent advances in image acquisition, processing and analysis now make it possible to quantify these patterns and dynamics to inform our understanding of urban growth, landscape evolution and environmental change. ⬠

Before Satellites: Favelas as Self-Organising Systems: Rio de Janeiro and São Paulo

Favelas are informal urban developments that occupy vacant private and public land. They are the creative efforts to build self-help housing of people who can only bank on their own initiative. In Brazil, favelas house between 20 and 40 per cent of the population of the country's major cities. They are the result of the failure of the national government's housing programme, and were generally ignored by central government as they had no legal basis in landownership. The Peruvian economist Hernando de Soto considers the political and social isolation of the favelas as a form of 'legal apartheid', and central government the 'greatest enemy of the migrants'.

To cope with this situation, favela migrants organised themselves to provide water and electricity, as well as to treat sewage in septic tanks. In addition to continually improving their own homes, inhabitants created social organisations with youth and sports programmes. Small-scale entrepreneurs provided services such as barber shops, a radio station or cafés in their homes, while many inhabitants raised poultry for food in cages on building roofs or in yards.

More recently, these self-organising groups reached out to the pioneering city of Rio Prefecture to analyse their demands and initiatives. As a result, the prefecture, and architect Lúcia Petersen, organised the Favela Bairro Programme, sponsoring competitions for the larger structures required in the favelas, and attracting the attention of socially conscious architects. The Harvard Graduate School of Design awarded the 2001 Veronica Rudge Green Prize in Urban Design to Jorge Mario Jáuregui for his work in different favelas in and around Rio de Janeiro. Also, in São Paulo, architect Renata Semin helped the Favela Heliópolis community association articulate its programmes and build a sports club and cultural centre in 1999–2000.

The 'urbanisation' of favelas is politically essential because it has a direct effect on the ground, improving inhabitants' lives and granting them a place in the city structure. This means the incorporation of the invisible 20 to 40 per cent of Brazilian urban inhabitants and their social organisations within the larger political economy. The exemplary Brazilian national City Statute 10.257 ('Estatuto da Cidade') will normalise the legal status of the favelas by granting the inhabitants ownership of the land under their house plots and compensating the previous owners. In addition, the plan will introduce basic infrastructure (water and sewerage) and social services (health care and so on).

For the favela dwellers, the Estatuto da Cidade forms the constitutional basis for their recognition as citizens, and rewards their prolonged struggle for an active role in city politics. Examples of these self-organising groups' projects are illustrated here, along with photographs from our book *FavelaMetropolis* (Birkhäuser, 2004). Architects played a variety of roles in support of self-organising community groups not all of which sought legal recognition, as some groups still prefer to retain their independence.

Favela Heliópolis radio station, São Paulo, Brazil
João Miranda, president of the self-organised community association UNAS, and radio-station staff. The station is a nucleus of favela activity.

Renata Semin, Piratininqa Arquitetos Associados, Favela Heliópolis sports and cultural centre, São Paulo, Brazil, 1999–2000
The architects designed and realised the sports and cultural centre for the UNAS community association within its favela context.

Favela Parque Royal, Rio de Janeiro, Brazil
Self-built housing along the seafront, with electrical supply meters.

Paulo Bastos, Favela de Jardim Imbuias, São Paulo, Brazil, 1996
An open stream before intervention from the architect, and after with high banks to prevent flooding.

Paulo Bastos, Favela Jardim Floresta, São Paulo, Brazil, 1996–8
Renovated side roads, stairs and ramps for pushcarts.

Archi 5 Arquitetos Associados, Favela Parque Royal, Rio de Janeiro, Brazil, 1995–7
A barber shop in a residential building with shops and services.

URBAN FIELD GUIDE

BALTIMORE, MARYLAND

APPLYING SOCIAL FORESTRY OBSERVATION
TECHNIQUES TO THE EAST COAST MEGALOPOLIS

A changing economy and different
lifestyles have altered the meaning of the
forest in the Northeastern United States,
prompting scientists to reconsider the
spatial form, stewardship and function of
the urban forest. Erika Svendsen, Victoria
Marshall and Manolo F Ufer describe
how social observation techniques and
the employment of a novel, locally based,
participatory hand-held monitoring
system could aid the exposure of more
positive socially orientated patterns of
land use.

Baltimore Ecosystem Study digital mosaic, 1999
The northeast megalopolis inhabits a giant hardwood forest as new houses carve
sites at the periphery of the older coastal cities. A bird's-eye view of the rapidly
suburbanising headwaters of the Gwynns Falls watershed in metropolitan Baltimore
is shown here in a false-colour infrared aerial photograph. The red colours indicate
active vegetation. Other colours represent streets, roofs and bare soil.

1. FORESTRY
Map, Talk and Record

On 13 August 1962, Bill Burch set out at dusk to observe visitors to the Rainbow Camp, in southern Oregon's Winema National Forest. He stayed in the camp, watching the activities, until 10 pm. The following morning, Burch returned to conduct daytime observations. He recorded a range of activities from sunbathing to chopping wood. Observations were confirmed through conversation rather than formal interview. Women approached along the trails often confirmed that they were 'searching for a rest room'. While men claimed to be in the woods to fish and hunt,

the forest, long managed for commodity production, had begun to shift to a landscape for home, work and play. From Burch we learn that human interactions with landscape processes contributed to newly emergent natural systems. In a reflective examination of ecological theory at the end of the 20th century, landscape historian William Cronon revealed that the earlier historical bias of ecologists had prevented a full understanding of the positive role of humans in promoting ecological change.[5]

2. THE URBAN FOREST
Street-Corner Interactions: Baltimore and New Haven

Another legacy of the pioneering work by Burch and his colleagues

Vacant lot, near Mount and Fayette streets, Franklyn Square, Baltimore
Throughout the northeast, shifts in urban population densities and economies disrupt the flow of critical resources such as social and financial capital, creating vacant patches of land. Self-organising systems such as drug dealing, rubbish dumping and invasive flora take over this area of the urban forest located in the southwest Baltimore neighbourhood of Franklin Square.

First day in Ms Shirley's garden
In the summer of 1993, for the first time in many years nearly a hundred children from the neighbourhood summer camp began to redirect the flow of energy and exchange on this same patch in Franklin Square. The children produced new space by appropriating the use and meaning of the vacant properties along Fayette and Mount streets as a garden. In this image the sidewalk becomes a performed garden path.

Burch later observed that only a small percentage of time was spent engaged in these particular sports. Rather, he found these same men to be enjoying less directed activities such as collecting pine cones, reading, rock throwing and socialising. A few more days of research revealed that children were the driving force in the forest: parents were led through the forest as a result of their explorations. And so it went until the entire camp ground, serving as an ecological/administrative unit, was mapped with a detailed inventory including vehicle state-licence plates, popular sunbathing rocks, meditation points and informal trails.[1]

Sixty-five years after the establishment of the US Forest Service, it is highly likely that William R Burch Jr was the first employed to apply Lynch's 'wayfinding'[2] and Jacobs' 'street ballet'[3] to forest dynamics. For years, ecologists had followed the mantra of *Man and Nature* (1864), in which George Perkins Marsh suggests that humans are not only separated from nature, but disrupt the self-regulating states of natural equilibrium.[4] The bias separating humans from ecological systems was fully exposed in the 1960s, as

at the Yale School of Forestry and Environmental Studies in the city of New Haven was a method of combining silviculture techniques with socioecological observations and casual conversation – the 'working circle plot'. In a recent interview, Bill Burch confessed that one of the great pains of his life was how 'the horticulturalist hijacked urban ecology'. The working circle method begins with the individual and household unit and connects to larger units of social organisation. It is the ecology *of* the city, rather than ecology *in* the city. While this early 1970s programme may appear similar to the urban horticultural movement, there is a distinct difference in scale and scope. Implicit in the approach is the knowledge that humans are not supraspecies, but, rather, an integrated part of urban ecology. Though it began in New Haven, the programme later spread to Nepal, Bhutan and China. The approach begins from the street corner and connects back out to the traditional forest stand.

An example of the working circle method is the corner of Mount and Fayette streets in southwest Baltimore, which in the 1980s became known as a notorious centre of drug activity.[6] It was also a critical cross-street for neighbourhood children as they passed by, daily, on their way to school, to the corner shop and to the community-managed recreation centre. A staggering number of

> Trees were planted in back alleys and fallow niches to redirect circulation patterns. Gardens were built on corner plots to signify change, as well as to induce a new rhythm of land use and programme.

urban ecological discourse. Disturbance, understood as an event that interrupts the relationship between organisms and their environment, typically radiates beyond the point of impact, and resilience is a natural part of system reorganisation after a disturbance.[7] An example is a forest or prairie where disturbance from fire can actually help stabilise, or even improve overall system health. In a city, disturbance can generate feelings of anxiety and stress causing instability. These feelings can often affect social and economic choices, with populations mourning for a lost neighbourhood or way of life. Disturbance often reveals underlying strengths and weaknesses that, unmitigated, are

Getting started
Children from the Franklin Square summer-camp programme began the work of building this garden in full view of neighbourhood residents as well as close to local drug activities. A new flow of energy is released, connecting critical resources such as land, labour and beliefs.

In full swing
These simple efforts later inspired neighbourhood adults to work towards a unified action of expanding the garden, for example planting trees and creating a new playground. In addition, institutional reforms led to new social programmes. Together, changes in the social production of physical space and behaviours prompted a significant change in the social organisation of the Franklin Square community.

vacant plots and abandoned houses created a porous environment, making it difficult to separate these modes of activity. By the early 1990s, community activists were working alongside student foresters from the Urban Resources Initiative (URI) to observe, inventory, map and devise a landscape strategy for the distinct pathways, plots and alleys used for both drug activity and as children's outdoor play areas. The Department of Recreation and Parks delivered massive amounts of soil for replanting. Trees were planted in back alleys and fallow niches to redirect circulation patterns. Gardens were built on corner plots to signify change, as well as to induce a new rhythm of land use and programme.

The neighbourhood recreation centre developed initiatives to monitor, manage and maintain this emergent urban forest habitat. Although it slowly fell into disrepair as neighbourhood leaders passed away or moved out, a few trees remain and traces of the gardens are still visible. Upon reflection years later, a long-time resident commented: 'At that time, it seemed like anything was possible.'

Disturbance and Resilience
The effects of urban greening in the city can be understood within cycles of disturbance and resilience that exemplify contemporary

merely reinforced in the next stage of succession. Humans are a critical part of mitigating disturbance and it is here that urban greening works. Human societies have the unique ability to be reflexive and manage levels of abstraction that can create positive externalities such as freedom of expression, building trust and creating social equity. Local–global interactions shape these resilient processes, or 'feedback loops', constraining and enabling group identities, social networks and shared values.

Metaphor and Feedback
Contemporary urban ecologists have called for integrated concepts to enliven the conceptual framework of 'feedback loops'.[8] Metaphors are useful communication tools that reveal hidden meanings about space. The term 'visual field' is a metaphor that emerges from observations of land where one's field of vision automatically defines a boundary around what can be seen. Visual fields, according to linguistics scholars Lakoff and Johnson, are containers.[9] Imagine the East Coast Megalopolis as a string of cities within a forest. This vision triggers a new image of a city

where everyday decisions are made within a new feedback loop: how to manage a dynamic, constructed, inhabited forest? The first step in forest management is being able to identify critical system processes. For this reason, social foresters do not count trees; rather, they look for interactions, exchanges and resilient processes that hold this inhabited forest together. Their goal is to uncover critical processes that often remain hidden from our core understanding of everyday life. In this scenario, the forest still exists even when one cannot see it, for it appears in our social actions, meanings, words, street-level exchanges and even mode of dress.

flow of water. Rubbish sheds, health sheds or kid sheds are suggested, in this context, to be critical social catchment areas defined by the ability, analogous to the flow and exchange cycles of a watershed, to capture materials, information and energy.

A social forester feedback loop has the unique potential to identify and link these emergent invented garden traditions with management of sheds or patches, towards a hybrid form of stewardship, which may be more equitable, innovative and responsive than traditional urban environmental management. This could allow a metaphorical urban ecological imagination to emerge, so that we are all 'thinking like a forest', no matter where we are.

Ms Shirley's reward
Changes in the meaning of urban space led to a change in social identities for many of the residents of Franklin Square. Ms Shirley's garden (Ms Shirley is pictured here with local children) became both a symbol and a dynamic driver of this identity change – a symbol of neighbourhood resilience and of a respected community leader.

Work in progress
After the first summer, there was still more work to be done in Franklin Square. A work in progress is essential to the process and cycle of resilience. A finished project suggests that the cycle has ended. Greening projects, which are replete with new improvisations, become incubators of emergent and diverse forms of civil society.

3. SCALING UP
Gardens, Parks and Hybrid Governance

Gardens are often the most obvious local starting point for human action in response to a disturbance, and also the most obvious starting point for the work of social foresters. Traditional park typologies have captured only those sites that have vegetation. However, five park types have been defined in the US since 1850: the pleasure ground, reform park, recreation facility, open-space system and, the most contemporary model, the sustainable park. For us, the open-space system continues to hold great force as a conceptual model. It occurred around 1965 when 'recreation came to be seen as something that could take place anywhere – in the streets, on a rooftop, at the waterfront, along an abandoned railway line as well as in traditional plazas and parks'.[10]

Urban greening, understood as an 'invented garden tradition', is nested within the dynamic and emergent open-space system.[11] New ways have been found to expand urban greening for research and monitoring, building on the notion of a watershed – the topographical area that catches the

Urban greening, understood as an 'invented garden tradition', is nested within the dynamic and emergent open-space system. New ways have been found to expand urban greening for research and monitoring, building on the notion of a watershed – the topographical area that catches the flow of water.

The Field Guide and Advance Spotters

How can urban resilience and feedback be accelerated in the 21st century, given that social ecologists, economists and epidemiologists have found that all systems are 'leaky', particularly at the stage of reorganisation? 'What is lost and what is gained' through reorganisation is traditionally measured in a single time scale or filtered through certain power narratives. To reconceive this 'leaky' dynamic, we have imagined a new role for social foresters.

As 'advance spotters' they will operate under a new protocol of the Urban Field Guide. In a twist to performing duties similar to that of the forest ranger stationed on the prairie or in forest-fire towers, advance spotters are charged with monitoring typically unseen processes occurring in rapidly changing environments at ground level. Through hand-held devices and satellites, advance-spotter observations could be fed into larger databases used by natural resource agencies, which would also be available for use in the field by spotters. Using GPS technology, spots can be located, photographed, described and uploaded in real time. Unlike when observing fish or plants or molecules, spotters can talk to people. Casual conversations and interviews, as used by Burch in the camp, serve to confirm observations.

An advance spotter will be able to identify patches of the urban forest charged with a collective memory, common enjoyment, places that enable trust and equity to emerge as social interactions in response to flows of water, space, light, vegetation,

Girl with evergreen
By 1999, the tree, the girl and the fence no longer exist at the corner of Mount and Fayette streets in Franklin Square. This suggests the fragile nature of such efforts. The role of the 'advance spotter' is to amplify and connect to another scale of interaction in order to defend and legitimise these efforts within the urban forest. At the same time, these actions exist in the collective memory of the urban forest, and similar efforts are now under way just a few blocks away.

waste and information. The advance spotter, acting within a feedback loop, can choose to continually monitor and observe emergent processes or respond to them, for example, becoming an interactive agent with others, sharing, amplifying, defending, inventing or resisting. To derive patterns from a study of processes, rather than to ascribe processes to observed patterns, is an ecological approach.[12] The Urban Field Guide is, therefore, not only a tool to gather information over time, but also has a role in translating the information into a legible 4-D map – one that allows time to be sorted in simultaneous and multiple ways. In this way, indirect (or leaky) effects can be made legible, tracked and, in turn, responded to. Over time, advance-spotter feedback accelerates, enabling us to become sensitive to the time scales, activities, various forms, sounds, noises, smells and feel of the electronic urban forest. 4

Advance spotter log

Using technology and social forest theory, 'advance spotters' can capture these landscapes of resilience over time and space by mapping the social catchment areas, such as kid sheds, of a larger watershed. The intent is to go beyond creating a collective memory of the invented garden, but to harness the capacity of civil society and government to restore critical feedback loops essential to the larger scales of the forest megalopolis

Available from www.urbanfieldguide.net

Advance spotter map

The entire US northeastern megalopolis is reconceived as a forest system. Critical emergent forest processes of trust, legacy, symbiosis and power have been identified by the 'advance spotter' in this particular time-series rendering of the system. Each spot is recorded with a time-sensitive point. Brighter points and longer lines are recent entries. This prototype is accessible as a real-time, multiscalar web site. The map is designed to be downloadable as a GIS navigational tool for street-level spotting, and uploadable for spotter entries.

Notes

1 William WR Burch Jr, *Observation: As a Technique for Recreation Research*, USDA Forest Service, Pacific Northwest Forest and Range Experiment Station,1964.
2 In *The Image of the City*, urban theorist Kevin Lynch uses 'wayfinding' to explore the relationship between human cognition and urban form. Lynch suggests that humans create mental maps to 'image' the structure of the large-scale city. Wayfinding is navigated by five basic elements: districts, paths, edges, nodes and landmarks. Kevin Lynch, *The Image of the City*, Cambridge Technology Press (Cambridge, MA), 1960, p 196.
3 In *The Death and Life of Great American Cities*, urban theorist Jane Jacobs recognised that street life and public space fostered critical interactions between strangers. In this sense, the city streets are incubators of emergent and diverse forms of social interaction. Jacobs refers to this as the 'street ballet'. Jane Jacobs, *The Death and Life of Great American Cities*, Random House (New York), 1961.
4 George Perkins Marsh, *Man and Nature*, C Scribner (New York), 1864.
5 William J Cronon, 'The turn toward history', in MJ McDonnell and STA Pickett (eds), *Humans as Components of Ecosystems: The Ecology of Subtle*

Human Effects and Populated Areas, Springer-Verlag (New York), 1993, pp VII–XI.
6 David Simon and Edward Burns, *The Corner: A Year in the Life of an Inner-City Neighbourhood*, Broadway Books (New York), 1997.
7 Lance H Gunderson and CS Holling, *Panarchy: Understanding Transformations in Human and Natural Systems*, Island Press (Washington DC) 2002.
8 STA Pickett, RS Ostfield, M Shachak and GE Likens (eds), *The Ecological Basis of Conservation: Heterogeneity, Ecosystems, and Biodiversity*, Chapman & Hall (New York), 1997, and Simon Levin, *Fragile Dominion: Complexity and the Commons*, Perseus Books (Reading, MA), 1999.
9 George Lakoff and Mark Johnson (eds), *Metaphors We Live By*, University of Chicago Press, 2003.
10 Galen Cranz and Michael Boland, 'Defining the sustainable park: A fifth model for urban parks', *Landscape Journal*, Vol 23, No 2, September 2004, pp 102–20.
11 John Dixon Hunt, 'The garden as cultural object', in Stuart Wrede and Howard Adams (eds), *From Denatured Visions: Landscape and Culture in the Twentieth Century*, Museum of Modern Art (New York), 1991, p 19.
12 Ashwani Vasishth and David Slone, 'Returning to ecology: An ecosystem approach to understanding the city', in M Dear (ed), *From Chicago to LA – Making Sense of Urban Theory*, Sage Publications (London), 2002, pp 347–66.

Beyond Great Walls: Inner Mongolia

While the economies of China's coastal cities continue to grow at breakneck speed, vast swathes of the Inner Mongolian grasslands are degrading to desert wastelands.

The assault on the ecology of the region started a few decades ago, when Chinese (agri)cultural policies actively swamped Inner Mongolia with Han Chinese farmers and encouraged nomadic Mongol shepherds to settle down. Excessive cultivation gradually altered the hydrology of the highlands. Freshwater lakes and rivers dried out, ground-water tables dropped almost everywhere, wind erosion intensified. Each spring, increasingly aggressive sand storms blast through Beijing, and cover regions as far as the American Midwest with a blanket of dust and pollutants.

Struggling to feed a fifth of the world's population with only 7 per cent of the world's arable land, China cannot afford to take the affected land out of agricultural production. Withdrawal is not an option. Instead, Beijing has embarked on the second phase of the Shelterbelt Program, a massive tree-planting campaign in the northwest. The so-called Green Wall fits in with China's tradition of centrally planned engineering masterpieces, crafted by millions of 'volunteering' hands and backed by the Communist Party's propaganda machine. It is expected to 'combat desertification', 'bring protection' and 'force the deserts to retreat'.

An up-close view across Inner Mongolia confirms that the trees are not primarily intended to replace cleared forests, or to help the grasslands to recover. Don't be fooled by its colour – the Green Wall is as native to the grassland ecosystem as a highway, a cow, a fence, a cabbage field, a Mongolian-style tourist village or a mobile-phone mast. It is virtually everywhere in Inner Mongolia. In different shapes and sizes, it outlines the human footprint on the grass – millions of trees lining roads, protecting croplands and screening villages, chequerboard vegetation consolidating eroded hillsides.

As a result of (or despite) the size of the project, long-term effects of the Green Wall remain largely unclear. The affirmative combating of a dust bowl is a fairly new discipline, which worries most scientists. Beijing assures that 'by 2050, all reclaimable desertified land will have been brought under basic control', while the Chinese might be hearing less optimistic sounds through the cracks in the government's Great Firewall.

The Great Wall, the one in stone, repeatedly failed to protect the empire it enclosed. Genghis Khan is believed to have simply bribed the sentries. Still, it did have significant functions: subsequently it served as a road in difficult terrain, as a stone quarry and as big tourist business.

With a travel grant from SOM Foundation, Jan Leenknegt crossed northern China on a bicycle in the autumn of 2004 to take measurements of the desertification crisis in Inner Mongolia. The full report of this trip is available at www.janleenknegt.com/beyondgreatwalls.html.

Grasslands near Xilinhot, Inner Mongolia, China
'Grasslands: Areas of land too high or cold to support anything other than grass, and agriculturally useful only as pastureland for sheep or cattle. Found especially in Inner Mongolia, Qinghai and Xinjiang.' (Glossary, *Geology Guide China*)
Inset: White areas show distribution of grasslands in China.

The upper reaches of the Xiliao He River, Xilinhot Prefecture, Inner Mongolia, China
'A report by a US embassy official in May 2001 after a visit to the Xilinhot Prefecture (x) notes that although 97 per cent of the region is officially classified as grasslands, a third of the terrain now appears to be desert. Researchers say that if recent desertification trends continue, Xilinhot Prefecture will be uninhabitable in 15 years.' (Lester Brown, www.earth-policy.org/Updates.Update26.htm)
Inset: White areas show distribution of desertification affected lands in China.

The Great Wall of China
Paranoically trying to adapt to shifting boundaries and changing threats, the Great Wall of China took shape as a collection of roughly parallel segments rather than a single protective wall. This masterpiece of shortsightedness, built by successive inward-looking dynasties (Qing and Han full line, Ming dotted), spanned many more miles than strictly 'needed', yet never adequately protected the empire. The wall used to separate two diametrically opposed cultures: to the south, Chinese farmers in the fertile valleys of Hebei, and to the north, Mongolian seminomadic shepherds on the highlands. Situated roughly between the Great Wall and the Sino-Mongolian border, Inner Mongolia (IM) was established in 1947 as the first Autonomous Region in the People's Republic.

Not only on the larger scale, a master plan for the construction of the Great Walls was lacking. A close-up view of the wall shows a haphazard construction method: layers of brick parallel to the slope randomly alternate with horizontal layers.

Beyond the Great Wall ... the Wild Northwest
'Zhangleanqi is just another unhospitable settlers' outpost – brand new factories on the outskirts, dust blasting through the town's oversized boulevards. As if Zhangleanqi was dropped off by a couple of trucks just a week ago. These cardboard towns will only get more depressing as I move on north, higher on the Mongolian plateau.' (Author's travel notes)

Private walls
Left: 'A Mongolian yurt is perfectly round not only to create the greatest space out of the least material, but also to stand up to the fierce katabatic winds, which whistle round it rather than topple it over.' (Dornod Sumber, www.economist.com/world/asia/displayStory.cfm?story_id=1487499)
Right: 'The traditional Chinese house is inward-facing and enclosed by a wall to provide shelter from the harsh winter winds.'
(http://depts.washington.edu/chinaciv/home/3intrhme.htm)

A farm near Sanggin Dalai, Inner Mongolia, China
'From the 1980s, Beijing privatised pasture through contracting-out. In Inner Mongolia (IM), fencing has gone up to delineate private land, while in Mongolia (M) one can still ride the 1,900 miles from west to east without encountering a single man-made impediment. As a result, Inner Mongolia and Mongolia are distinguishable from the air: up to 40 per cent of Inner Mongolia's grasslands are degraded, less than 10 per cent are in Mongolia. However, the question for Mongolia is how long a free-market economy can continue to coexist with public ownership of the land.' (Dornod Sumber, www.economist.com/world/asia/displayStory.cfm?story_id=1487499)
Inset: Distribution of degraded grasslands (dark green) in Mongolia (M) and Inner Mongolia (IM).

Mongolian heritage
On a hilltop outside Xilinhot, the Chinese authorities have erected copies of Lamaist stupas as a tribute to the Mongolian heritage of the region. Rarely visited by either Mongolians or Han Chinese, the site is an impressive monument to cynicism. While Mongolians gathered around those stupas to ask the gods for plentiful rainfall on the grasslands, the same Chinese authorities continue the assault on the hydrology of the region. No heritage without death.
Inset: The vast majority of China's desertified areas (white) are situated in the four so-called Autonomous Regions: Inner Mongolia (IM), Ningxia (N), Xinjiang (X) and Tibet (T), home to the Mongol, Hui, Uigur and Tibetan peoples respectively.

Samples of the Green Wall of China
Millions of trees line railways, fields and roads. 'Although forest clearing continues at a frightening rate, China's overall forest cover has recently risen to almost 14 per cent, mainly brought about by the Green Wall. Sadly, though, the biological value of these replanted forests is far lower than that of the natural forests they replace. Replanted forests can provide timber for industrial and household use, but do not adequately replace the role of natural forests in protecting soil, retaining water or supporting wildlife.' (*Rough Guide to China*, Rough Guides (London), 2003, p 1216)

Vegetation in chequerboard patterns to contain eroding soil along road 207A to Xilinhot, China
Chequerboard vegetation can be found on all scales, all over Inner Mongolia. 'Mao's principles held that constant struggle was part of existence, and thus that acceptance of the status quo was in itself a bad thing.' (*Rough Guide to China*, Rough Guides (London), 2003, p 1186)

A SURVEY OF THE TRANSCONTINENTAL GAS PIPELINE FROM HOUSTON TO NEW JERSEY

SURFACTANT SYSTEMS

The Transcontinental Pipeline, Transco, is a 10,560-mile line that traverses the US, transporting natural gas from its source in the Gulf of Mexico to the East Coast. **Petia Morozov** describes the postwar engineering feat that made the pipeline a reality, and also reveals the web of myriad agreements, with often diametrically opposed parties or interests, that support its rights of way and management.

An eerie stillness drifts along the western banks of Louisiana's Atchafalaya River. Except for the occasional robin signalling overhead, or centuries-old cypress trees rustling in a balmy wind, there is little evidence that one of America's most important pieces of energy infrastructure is rumbling underground at 11 miles per hour. In the distance stands one tower of a suspension bridge, painted white and elegantly poised against the backdrop of a tall, grassy levee. This place is magnificently void of any human inhabitation as two pipes, 30 inches in diameter, rocket out of the ground and triangulate with the piers of the structure, nearly 60 feet overhead. The pipes float in unison under an arch of tensioned cables, disappearing behind the embankment and heading towards the east.

Between the red state of Texas and the blue state of New Jersey, this hearty lifeline pulsates under a contentious geopolitical radar, in which torrents of gas gush through

Pipeline + Countries + Political Network

Pipeline + Waterbody Network

Pipeline + Gas Pipeline Network

Pipeline + Night Sky + Houston/NYC

Composite of all networks

Emergence
Transco's 3,650-foot suspension bridge spanning the Atchafalaya River in Louisiana was the longest natural-gas pipeline suspension bridge in the country at the time of its construction.

the nation's longest natural-gas line, the Transcontinental Pipeline. Ongoing building and managing of this 10,560-mile network of infrastructure – connecting the Gulf of Mexico's natural-gas fields to the financial capitals of the eastern seaboard – is a project of exchange between easement and owner, agent and steward, hinterland and wetland, visibility and security.

Known as Transco, the pipeline traverses 13 states and 200 counties, and encompasses more than 3,000 miles of right-of-way. Averaging 100 feet in width, this corridor comprises a rolling patchwork of more than 25,000 pieces of public and private property, of which its current holding corporation, Williams Company, owns only 1 per cent. It is a startling organisational feat that is managed in increments of days and seasons, individuals and corporations, saplings

National mappings
The Transco pipeline and various macro systems of organisation inform each other's routes of distribution in mutually modifying patterns.
At times, the pipeline courses through geologies without any apparent obstruction. At others, it surrenders to impassable hydrological systems.

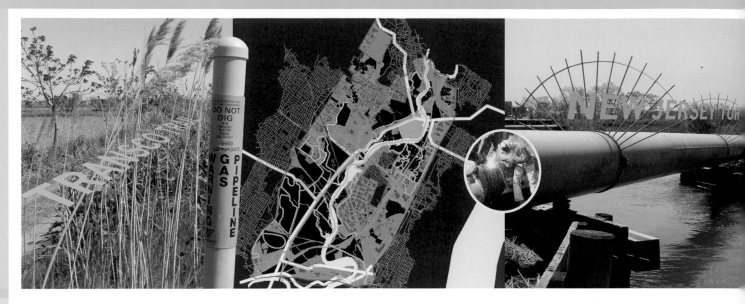

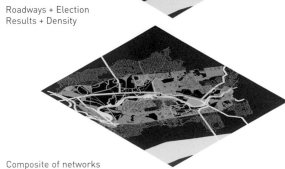

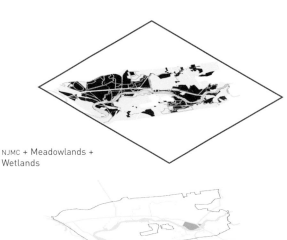

NJMC + Meadowlands + Wetlands

Pipeline + Mitigation Bank + Waterways

Roadways + Election Results + Density

Composite of networks

Local mappings
A close-up examination of the Transco pipeline as it enters various jurisdictional boundaries at local and regional geographies.

CASE STUDY

Williams Company soon formed a subsidiary enterprise called Marsh Resources in order to capitalise on its ownership of a 206-acre wetlands property in the Meadowlands and to designate it as a wetlands mitigation bank. The site has a 'service area' of the Hackensack River Drainage Basin, Newark Bay and the New Jersey banks of the Hudson River, and is being transformed from a degraded phragmites-choked system to a more natural intertidal, salt-marsh-estuarine, island/channel/mudflat ecosystem. Historically, the site was a complex wetland system that supported a diverse array of freshwater and estuarine plant and animal species. Over the last hundred years, overdevelopment and mosquito ditching has led to a total degradation of the site. Phragmites, an invasive reed, took over the site at the expense of all other plant species. This led to an overall loss of wetland functions and values, as well as eliminating the site's beneficial and desirable wildlife habitat. The bank was created to restore a low-value wetland area to its natural pristine state, and to generate wetland mitigation credits. The price for mitigation credits includes land cost, design, bank permits, construction, maintenance, agency negotiations for use of the bank and all ongoing monitoring requirements. Its current ratio of one credit per acre of wetland is considered this new industry's most desirable and most profitable ratio in the northeast.

The crowning achievement in cooperative strategies is considered by Williams to be a 1-mile section of pipeline and accompanying road that is successfully managed as a nature trail. This self-guided natural trail is located at the headquarters of the New Jersey Meadowlands Commission, a model supramunicipal organisation situated 6 miles west of New York, with planning jurisdiction over 14 towns (or 20,000 acres), and with a dual mandate of economic development and ecological preservation. The trail serves to connect an adjacent nature reserve with a floating trail through a restored salt marsh. Up to a thousand schoolchildren use the trail every month in order to participate in environmental education programmes.

The Meadowlands site also marks a rare moment in which the pipeline is in full view along both the turnpike and the trail, and suspended above the rich wet landscape. It emerges at the end of a long journey, lingering above the marshes as if to declare this unique triad of trail, pipeline and bank as a pre-eminent example of robust design strategies. This case study gives pause to imagine how similar networked systems can operate at incrementally greater scales, with the pipeline as the recurring physical and organisational backdrop.

and forests, town officials and federal commissioners. As the various actors converge upon this ongoing interplay of scales, time frames and constituencies, a new model of networking emerges to defy traditional planning strategies. A top-down view of the pipeline would suggest a pure and linear transect. However, the pipeline assumes an uncanny degree of imperceptibility, both physically and organisationally, that would irritate most sightseers and mystify most planners.

Steel<Fuel>Farm

In the aftermath of the Second World War, the us was actively exploiting wartime industries in steel manufacturing, oil extraction and agricultural techniques, and looking to transform these industries to capture new markets, both domestically and globally. Steel became the ubiquitous building material, farmers saw generous federal subsidies, and energy consumption was soaring across the country. Existing utility and transport infrastructures nationwide were pressured to adapt to the new order of global prosperity. It was then that a radical proposition to convert the old 'Inches' oil pipelines that once fuelled Europe-bound navy tankers emerged as an innovative adaptation of an existing interstate infrastructure. This plan – proposed by the Texas Eastern company – was quickly implemented by the Federal Energy Commission in 1945, and two years later the northeast got its first taste of a cleaner-burning energy supply. However, increased demand prompted the urgency to build another natural-gas pipeline and, in 1948, Claude Williams, owner of Transcontinental Gas Pipe Line (TGPL), was granted approval to build what would be – and still is – the longest pipeline in the country.

The pipeline was designed to originate in Hidalgo County, Texas, and terminate some 2,000 miles away in New York City. At the time it was built, Transco required the review of 9,000 pages of regulatory testimony, the raising of nearly $235 million in private funding, the manufacture of 520,000 tons of steel, easement negotiations with more than 8,000 landowners, and clearing of over 25,000 acres of forested and occupied land. Four prevailing issues of safety, security, easement access and easement negotiation dictated the design, location and implementation of the pipeline, and as such constrained Transco's siting to rural areas that expected to see slow population growth. Large-tract property owners such as farmers, foresters, highway authorities and other utility companies proved to be the most accommodating easement partners, despite the irony that they would be least likely to be Transco's customers. Their willingness to monitor their easements on a daily basis supplemented Transco's weekly aerial documentation.

The greatest opposition to the construction of the pipeline came from rapidly developing areas that were once agricultural – for example, from the people of Milltown in New Jersey, who were the pipeline's first gang of protesters – systematically rising to challenge, only to be defeated by, the jurisdictional authority of the pipeline's federal commissioners. Transco's interstate pipeline gave the company the regulatory backing of federal agencies and the trusted power of eminent domain in order to carry

out its mission. Despite this untouchable status, however, Transco quickly learned to dodge urban nodes whenever possible, selectively eliminating creative right-of-way opportunities for fear of public scrutiny and false impressions. In the absence of any federal land-use policies for the pipeline easement itself, designed features were limited to placement of pipeline markers, variations on the definition of allowable temporary structures and the creative interpretation of area occupancy rates.

Transco's first successful partnership came accidentally, when the pipeline was installed along the entire length of the New Jersey Meadowlands in order to reach New York City. Due to extreme wetland soil conditions encountered in portions of this area, it was necessary to construct expensive roadways along the pipeline to facilitate pipeline installation and maintenance. At the same time, the New Jersey Turnpike Authority was planning a direct north–south route through the state as part of Interstate 95, an immense highway project that would provide farming communities with greater access to urban populations in a reciprocal arrangement of goods distribution. The two entities engaged in a cooperative design approach that benefited both parties mutually, in which the Turnpike built the necessary roadway to the pipeline's storage facilities, and Transco supplied easement rights for the Turnpike. Finally, on 16 January 1951, the pipeline valves were officially opened between Texas and New York, and the promise of 300 years of fuel and a cleaner environment closed the economic gap between both regions of the country.

It is worth mentioning that only 10 years later, in 1961, Jean Gottmann's Megalopolis would characterise growth patterns emerging between Washington DC and Boston that 'may be considered the cradle of a new order in the organisation of inhabited space'. This work would help to establish urban theory somewhere between Benton Mackaye's 1928 nonlinear model of regional planning (the idealised culmination of the Appalachian Trail) and Joel Garreau's forthcoming edge cities model of settlement patterns in 1991 – the antithesis of the centralised urban plan.

Gottmann's exemplary 1961 analysis of the megapolitan phenomenon was not merely a forecast of emergent city growth, but a mapping of Transco's future market territories. In the same 40-year span, the pipeline would expand to nearly 10 times its original length and four times its capacity, outpacing any other mode of energy distribution in the world and forming the currency that would revolutionise globalisation and politicisation of a natural commodity. By the time the pipeline was purchased by Williams Company in 1995, the natural-gas market frenzy would earmark Houston – with its two giant energy conglomerates, Enron and Williams leading the pack – as the third largest city in the us, rivalling New York's financial prowess and Washington's political power.

Trail+Bank+Pipeline

In the early 1990s, the pipeline's purveyors began to explore possible partnerships with traditionally opposing agendas. With the regulatory culture seeking avoidance and mitigation, private interests clamouring for development in someone else's back yard, and special interest groups looking for ways to preserve and enjoy green space, it was necessary to at least consider opportunities to make their needs compatible with other interests. The handful of programmes that were implemented proved to be very positive, cost-effective and enjoyable. They included the use of cooperative agreements with landowners for right-of-way maintenance, memoranda of understanding with national conservation groups for vegetative management practices beneficial to wildlife, the granting of conservation easements on company-owned property, the dedication of portions of right-of-way as education and nature trails, and other innovative land-use programmes. These partnerships often resulted in direct benefits through cost savings and avoidance, and indirect ones through the advantages of strategic alliances and positive public relations.

Soon after the trail was built, the US Department of the Army Corps of Engineers, in conjunction with the Environmental Protection Agency, the Department of Agriculture (Natural Resources Conservation Service), the Department of the Interior (Fish and Wildlife Service) and the Department of Commerce (National Oceanic and Atmospheric Administration) issued a document in 1995 entitled 'Federal Guidance for the Establishment, Use and Operation of Mitigation Banks'. The federal guidance document defines mitigation banking as 'the restoration, creation, enhancement and, in exceptional circumstances, preservation of wetland, and/or other aquatic resources expressly for the purpose of providing compensatory mitigation in advance of authorised impacts to similar resources'.

In this new paradigm of land-use transaction, displaced wetlands property acts like currency in what are called mitigation banks, cleverly mobilising environmental conservation laws such as the Clean Water Act while promising like-kind exchange. The concept and implementation of wetland mitigation banking allows companies at risk of disturbing on-site wetlands to exchange and transplant units of land of one ecological make-up with something

entirely dissimilar – and in surprisingly remote relocations – in order to bypass strict environmental legislation.

ZoomIN=ZoomON=ZoomOUT

Lest one mistake the pipeline's easement for a public greenway between Houston and New York, it should be stated outright that it would be nearly impossible to travel on foot or by car. Unlike the Appalachian Trail – the linear national park that is delicately balanced along the crest of contiguous mountain ranges – the Mega-Transco Trail, were it to ever be called that, would require the likes of Lewis and Clark, whose combined strengths in cartography, water navigation, botany, geology, physical fitness and amicable negotiation were merely introductory skills for their cross-country expedition.

What makes navigating this pipeline tricky is the incessant swapping between two lines: that which is public – a network of roadways and unrestricted thoroughfares – and that which is private – a linear sequence of privately owned pipeline easements. Routes for daily monitoring drives look more like a cardiogram than a smooth line, intermittently running off course in a predictably random pattern before straightening out again. The easement is uncharted territory simply because it doesn't want to be noticed. Never mind the heightened need for national security, the easement is riddled with warnings, either in the form of barbed-wire fences or 'NO TRESPASSING' signs.

There is increasing pressure for Transco's rights-of-way to serve other interests besides those associated with the transmission of energy. While landowners, agencies and

←10
buildings

10–46
buildings

→46
buildings

Convergence

Today's pipeline-monitoring systems acquire redundant cataloguing of information from both the ground up and the top down. Satellite, aerial and in-field recording capabilities transport real-time data that extend well beyond the boundaries of the easement itself, and manage to track the week-to-week construction activities within a 660-foot radius along the easement's centreline. As part of the Department of Transportation's Office of Pipeline Safety regulations, each and every building must be accounted for within those easement parameters, whether a temporary or permanent structure. By assessing the number, occupancy and height of the structures, four classifications of pipe construction can be calculated, with Class I as the most rural category (and least constrained for pipe size, throughput and human risk) and Class IV as the most urban (and most constrained). Not surprisingly, Transco's only stretch of Class IV pipe construction occurs as it enters New York City's boundaries. With any class designation, the

burden is on the pipeline's owner to monitor construction of additional structures in order to determine whether class upgrades are required in certain areas. Very often, these monitoring practices also help to predict future development of an area, and its projected impact on pipeline upgrade and expansion. But what can such classifications mean for the physical manifestation of the pipeline's easement? Can these classes translate into some robust appraisal of the transect?

Class I   In response to rural conditions:
                 - Host to hunting clubs
                 - Seed harvesting, nurseries and greenhouse farming
                 - Strategic edge ecologies that promote biodiversity

other public entities expect this bisecting feature through the landscape to provide wildlife habitats, recreational and educational opportunities, other public and private benefits may also be compatible.

At Transco's 37 river crossings – including the Mississippi and Hudson rivers – the material incompatibilities between gas and water are revealed in the pipeline's construction methods. Whether elevated high above the river's tide, or anchored to its bottom in pressurised concrete-encased steel tubing, the serpentine transformation of the pipeline slyly avoids incidence with water at all cost. In its relentless trek south to north, it appears that an act of intolerance is rather a gesture of perverse accommodation, systematically subverting water fields into gas lines, and forcing us to function at the interface between the hydrophilic and the hydrophobic, the field and the line, the ground and the organisation. Perhaps this is just the first leg of a trip that, upon its return, brings back new models of social, economic and ecological distribution where our renewed understanding of these systems' related legacies of displacement help to invent the emulsified and transpolitan infrastructure. ⚙

As this issue goes to press, new urgencies in the aftermath of Hurricane Katrina are likely to challenge the distribution, management and land-use practices of the pipeline. It is the author's intention to present a framework that allows these future reconsiderations to emerge and to trigger the practice of alternative strategies, not in spite of the recent devastations, but because of them.

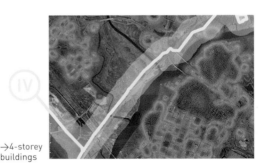

→4-storey buildings

Classes II / III   In response to emerging and saturated edge city conditions:
- Mid-scale greenbelt network
- Nonmotorised transport network for schools/business
- Mid-scale agricultural and seasonal enterprises

Class IV   In response to fully urbanised conditions:
- Multiscale networks of public amenities, trails, parks
- Small-scale agricultural enterprises
- Networked array of summer and winter gardens
- Alternative energy easements for solar and wind production

Megalopolis mappings
The Transco pipeline's management strategies straddle across various scales of surveillance resources within each of the pipeline's four monitoring divisions. This division stretches between New York City and Washington DC, or what Jean Gottmann referred to as the 'megalopolis'.

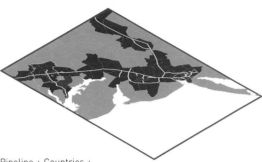

Pipeline + Countries + Election Results

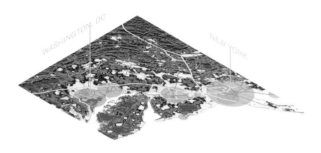

Pipeline + Interstates + Energy Use + Urban Nodes + Topography

Pipeline + Watersheds + Mitigation Areas + Farms

Composite of networks

Technopoles + Biotopes: Upstate New York

Technopoles are concentrated localisations of technologically innovative production that embrace different processes directly generated by information technologies and structured by the global economy. They pass over physical territorial boundaries, operate within multiple scales and time frames, and establish new relationships with urban places.

Borrowed from ecology, biotopes define self-regulating habitats for living things and their reiterative relationship between life (*bio*) and place (*topos*). Urban biotopes consist of an inclusive field that allows the understanding of territory as a complex adaptive system, exposing dynamic interactions between physical and nonphysical components.

Our question, in a design studio as part of the inaugural conference of the Upstate Institute at Syracuse University's School of Architecture, is how to direct a new Upstate New York technopole development towards neighbourhood revitalisation through a ring of hybrid interventions.[1] This work promotes the mutation and hybridisation of technopole and biotope models through splicing, analogously to generic recombination.[2] It involves the sorting, layering, overlapping and recombining of disparate elements to create new urban forms.

Urban actors, engaged in spatial mutation and hybridisation, create spaces for their activities in the layered matrix of the city. The studio radicalises the state-proposed upstate technopole within the flexible and evolutionary place of localised urban biotopes, leading to a new urbanity in downtown Syracuse. New node-places of social contact are between neighbourhoods and institutions as well as regional and downtown interests. Ultimately this work seeks to overcome the negative friction between the informational economy and the 'sense of place' embedded in the region's inhabitants.

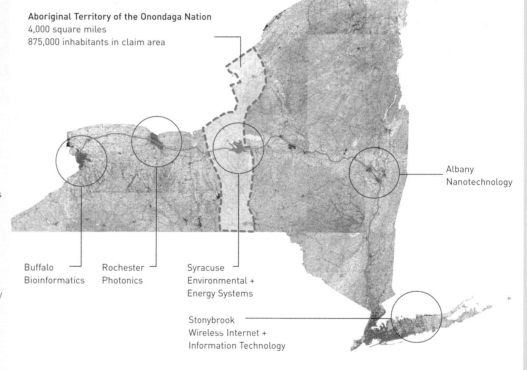

The Empire State High Tech-Corridor stretches from Long Island northwards to Albany and then west to Syracuse, Rochester and Buffalo (1).

The Erie Canal (opened in 1825, and was closed for commercial use in the 1950s) spurred the first great westward movement of American settlers, gave access to the land and resources west of the Appalachians, and made New York the pre-eminent commercial city in the US (2).

The Onondaga Nation currently claims ownership rights to a corridor of land extending from the Canadian border to the Pennsylvania border, including Onondaga County (3).

(1) http://coees.internetconsult.com/empire.aspx

(2) http://www.canals.state.ny.us/cculture/history/

(3) http://ongov.net/

Aboriginal Territory of the Onondaga Nation
4,000 square miles
875,000 inhabitants in claim area

Albany
Nanotechnology

Buffalo
Bioinformatics

Rochester
Photonics

Syracuse
Environmental +
Energy Systems

Stonybrook
Wireless Internet +
Information Technology

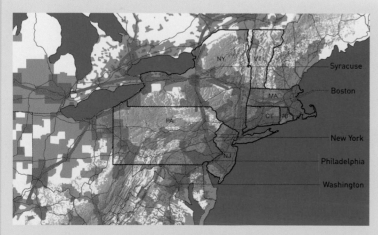

Location of Syracuse within the northeast megalopolis.

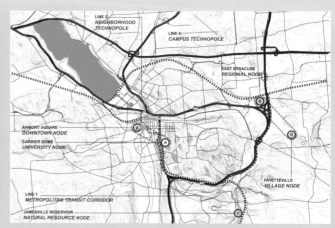

New regional nodes in the Syracuse metropolitan area.

Alessandro Cimini + Ignacio Lamar

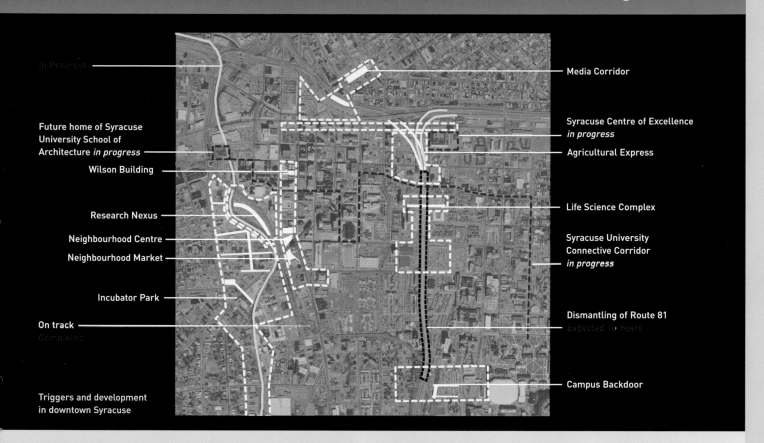

In Progress

Media Corridor

Future home of Syracuse University School of Architecture *in progress*

Syracuse Centre of Excellence *in progress*

Agricultural Express

Wilson Building

Research Nexus

Life Science Complex

Neighbourhood Centre

Neighbourhood Market

Syracuse University Connective Corridor *in progress*

Incubator Park

On track

Dismantling of Route 81
Expected 10 Years

Completed

Campus Backdoor

Triggers and development in downtown Syracuse

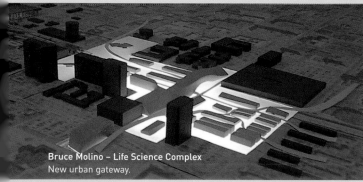

Bruce Molino – Life Science Complex
New urban gateway.

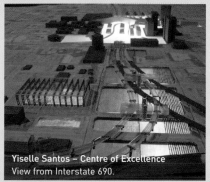

Yiselle Santos – Centre of Excellence
View from Interstate 690.

Charles Berg – Agricultural Express
View from experimental fields towards lab building.

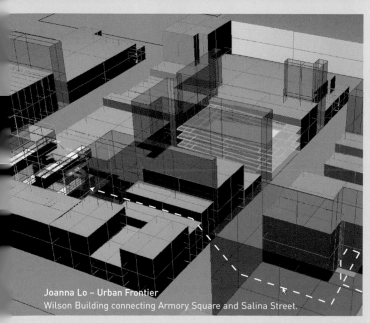

Joanna Lo – Urban Frontier
Wilson Building connecting Armory Square and Salina Street.

James Wene – Incubator Park
Riparian zone.

Notes

1 Spring 2005 Visiting Critic Studio led by Lawrence Davis, Brian McGrath and the authors with proposals for the 'UPSTATE: downtown' symposium presented by the School of Architecture under the direction of Dean Mark Robbins. Students: Nereeline Aragon, Charles Berg, Andreas Karales, Nartano Lin, Joanna Lo, Andrew Lynn, Bruce Molino, Todd Rowland, Yiselle Santos, Joshua Seidner, Desiree Seilhamer and James Wene.
2 Recombination is the process of crossing over an independent assortment of new combinations of genes in progeny that did not appear in the parents. See Grahame Shane, *Recombinant Urbanism: Conceptual Modelling in Architecture, Urban Design and City Theory*, John Wiley & Sons (London), 2004.

As the digital revolution deepens and pervades every aspect of daily life, virtual realities begin to penetrate one another in a multiplicity of ways. The amount of sensing data being compiled on the city grows, enabling the construction of virtual realities that can, in turn, be transformed for diverse purposes. Here, Michael Batty and Andrew Hudson-Smith from the

URBAN SIMULACRA
LONDON

Centre for Advanced Spatial Analysis, University College London, outline how they went about the construction of a virtual city in central London. A conventional 3-D-GIS/CAD model was used as the basis on which to build a digital realm in which designers are cast as avatars and populations as agents, so as to define new ways in which to understand and plan the city.

Replacing Foster and Partners' Swiss Re headquarters building in London with a composite New York skyscraper.

URBAN SIMULACRA
LONDON

1. Virtual Cities

Jean Baudrillard (1994) defines a simulacrum as a 'simulation of a simulation', a model of a model if you like.[1] In terms of cities in the digital realm, it is easy to translate such a conception into multiple layers of abstraction that we build up from the raw data we sense, perceive and explain in simulating urban form and structure. A generation or more ago, when computers were first used to represent cities, typical simulations were immediate and direct. Either the geometry of the city was used to construct digital 'iconic' models through which one could navigate, and sometimes use for CAD (computer-aided design), or geographic and economic functions were represented using 'symbolic' mathematical models that could be analysed and manipulated for the same ends: better design, better planning. As the digital revolution has matured, these conceptions have blurred, and now there are mathematical models that sit within iconic models, and vice versa, whose symbology exists on many levels. More importantly, perhaps, as computers have come to be used in everything from extracting data remotely, to mining it to find new

viewing the data – one perspective on the virtual city – and there are many others that need not stress the spatial dimension nor its built form. We construct this model as a series of data layers that we can overlay in 3-D. We can then embellish the model, adding a variety of digital media that we can deliver and display in everything from web browsers to holographic-like displays.

Such models can also be imported into other digital media. We illustrate the conception of a simulacrum by embedding it within a virtual world – a virtual design studio or exhibition space – which users can enter as avatars and then view and manipulate the model in the presence of other users, who are also avatars. This embedding can be recursive in that we can enter such worlds, view the model and then fly through it, adding new digital media at points where we need to render the environment with different images. Like many of our simulacra, Virtual London is designed so that users can learn about and redesign their environment in a

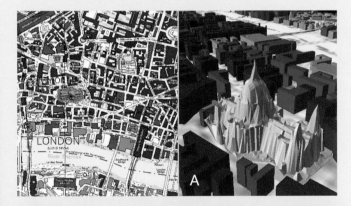

A

B

Figure 2: Building the virtual city in layers from the ground up. (a) Extruding parcel data to average height and inserting a LIDAR image of St Paul's Cathedral into the scene. (b) Adding a digital panorama of the area around the Swiss Re headquarters building.

Figure 1: View west from Tower Bridge across Virtual London, showing the raw geometry of the virtual city before it is populated with data.

patterns, visualising it in diverse ways, modelling it for the same diversity, and embedding users virtually into the process of use, models have come to be represented within models, worlds within worlds, as the power of recursive digital construction has gathered pace. This is simulacra: virtual cities within virtual cities where such embedding twists the process in curious but illuminating ways.

We will begin by describing the construction of a digital iconic model of central London that we somewhat euphemistically refer to as 'Virtual London'. Virtual London is in fact a 3-D geographic information system (3-D-GIS), which is in essence a large spatial database that can be analysed and queried. We can view it in 3-D because we can hold and file the data via digital representation of streets and building blocks. However, this is just one way of participatory sense. However, this also requires more formal analytical techniques – symbolic or mathematical models. To this end we will also illustrate how people as agents can be represented within the model, and how users can view these agents in using such models for solving real-world problems that, in turn, can be visualised within the wider Virtual London model. Our vision of the virtual city is thus one of many penetrating virtual worlds, from the world of data to the world of agents moving within the world, to the world of end-users manipulating the environment with other users in a participatory context.

2. Virtual London: Navigating and Analysing in 3-D using GIS, CAD and Multimedia

The most obvious of virtual cities is based on the geometry of the city that we represent as streets and buildings and compose in layers. An image of our model, which includes 45,000 buildings or blocks over 20 square

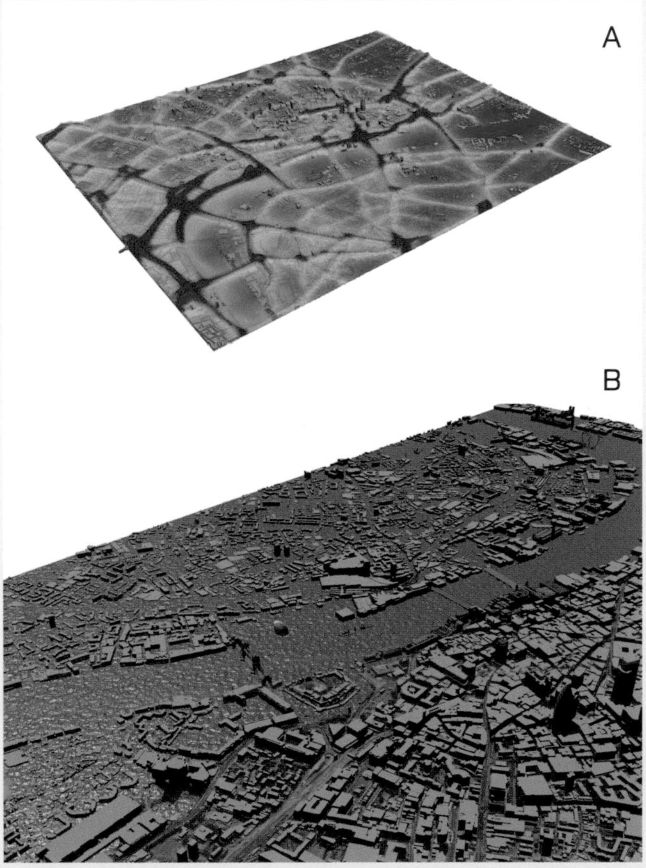

model (the building blocks) with data, ranging from building populations, air pollution along the streets, financial data such as rents and property taxes, social conditions such as crime rates, analyses of the impact of tall buildings in terms of locations from where they can be seen, the energy associated with building masses, employment, diversity of building use, and so on. We can also embed within the model other multimedia – for example, digital panoramas that record the 'real' detail of the city more superficially, yet also more directly – at any point where such detail might enhance the experience. And of course we can render each building in as much detail as we like, as demonstrated by the fish-eye view in Figure 2(b).

Examples of the applications described above are illustrated in Figure 3, in which we have 'flooded' the model with new layers of data. The figure shows how a visualisation of pollution, based on the particulate nitrogen oxide (mainly associated with vehicle emissions), can be layered as a surface onto the geometry. It also shows what would happen if the sea level rose 10 metres, which is equivalent to a rise in sea level in the North Atlantic if the

A

B

Figure 3: Populating the virtual city. (a) Adding a layer of pollution based on nitrogen oxide. (b) Flooding the model to a 10-metre rise in sea level.

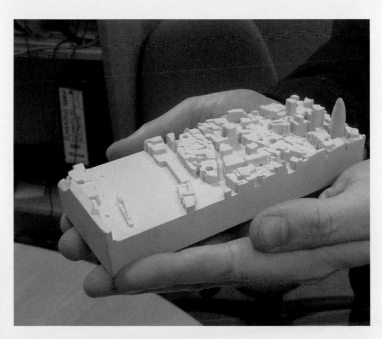

Figure 5: Back to 'the material world': printing a little bit of Virtual London.

kilometres, is shown in Figure 1. Building starts with a digital terrain model – the bare earth. Onto this is draped an aerial photograph. We then lay out the digital street and parcel map, then extrude the parcels to their average heights using LiDAR[2] data – clouds of x-y-z points defining the third dimension generated from low-flying aircraft using lasers that scan the geometry of the city as they fly across it. Figure 2(a) shows an example of this for St Paul's Cathedral. We can then populate this basic-skeleton

Greenland ice cap were to melt. However, more traditionally the model can be used to assess the visual impact of tall buildings on the surrounding area. In Figure 4 (see pp 42–3) we replace Norman Foster's new Swiss Re building (the 'Gherkin') in the City of London with a composite New York skyscraper, illustrating the impact of such a change in scale. Using a 3-D-GIS, we can compute the viewsheds from every place to any other, thus assessing the impact of relaxing the low-buildings policy that has dominated central London for the last 50 years.

This traditional virtual city model, conceived now as a 3-D view of a large spatial database, can be connected back to the sensing of data in real time – for example, to the air-pollution monitors used to generate Figure 3(a) – using new forms of distributed computing such as the 'grid'. But we can also connect the digital model back to more traditional icons. Just as we can print a paper copy from a GIS, or a static 3-D image from a CAD model, we can print a hard copy of the digital city in material terms.

In Figure 5, we have printed a little bit of Virtual London (an area around the Gherkin) using a CAD/CAM printer. This took two days to print or, rather, 'mill-out', but in the future this type of operation will become routine. Connecting peripherals such as sensing and printing devices (the most obvious being web cams) to the digital model is thus becoming more routine. Once we have such a structure, we can then port it to other worlds and it is to these that we now turn.

3. The Recursive Virtual World: Avatars in Panoramic Space

Any digital media can be embedded within any other digital environment – different from the one in which it is created, displayed or accessed – the simplest of such embeddings being those into web pages or portals. Slightly more elaborate and distributed environments might comprise a virtual world – a virtual exhibition space or room – into which one might enter perhaps as an avatar. Being able to control one's digital presence allows one to navigate the room and, if the model is displayed therein, also navigate the model. In a sense, this is the same kind of navigation that might be played out in the more direct form of virtual city described above, but in the virtual world it is much easier to associate with other users whose digital presence can also be displayed as avatars in the same scene. Avatars are, of course, coordinated, and can interact via the model, initiating dialogues about the environment or regarding issues such as design or problem-solving.

Such a picture of our virtual world is shown in Figure 6. It is based on porting the model into a virtual exhibition space, with users logging on from different places on the Net entering the scene, and then engaging in dialogue – interacting in ways that are close to the traditional uses of real iconic city models. We can also manipulate the scale and add other kinds of media. Figure 7 shows an avatar astride the digital model at a much greater scale, moving within a digital panorama overlooking the 'square mile' in the City of London, and walking within a 'cathedral'. After first first choosing a persona (see Figure 8), avatars begin to explore the world. Figure 9 shows how all this can be stitched together in a virtual world within which a virtual city is positioned, embedded with more realistic shots from panoramas, and incorporating various ways in which users can engage in dialogue, as well as ways in which data can be imported from the real 'real' world, through various sensors and web cams. This represents a future where all these channels, and more, will come to be fashioned and linked through virtual environments.

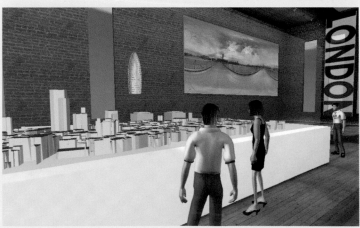

Figure 6: Entering the virtual world. Avatars engage with each other and with the virtual city in diverse ways.

Figure 7: Scaling the virtual world and adding digital panoramas as a backdrop.

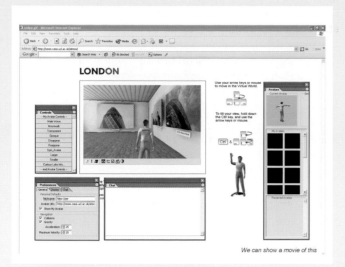

We can show a movie of this

Figure 8: Manipulating a persona and entering a virtual world populated as an exhibition of the virtual city.

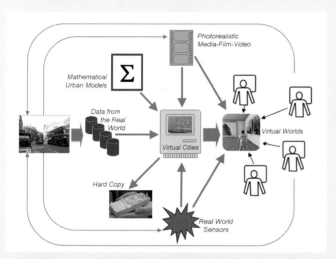

Figure 9: Deriving raw data from the real world and stitching it into virtual cities and virtual worlds.

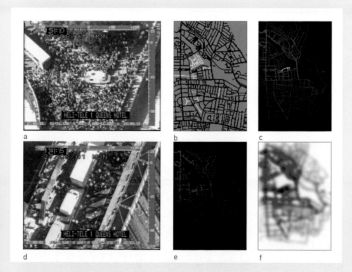

Figure 10: Embedding mathematical models into the virtual city.
(a) and (b) Crowds and the parade at the Notting Hill Carnival.
(c) The street system. (d) Agents moving around the carnival.
(e) The density of flow. (f) Crowding hot spots.

4. Agents as Well as Avatars Enter the Scene

The last twist in our tale is when we begin to import more mathematically inspired models into our virtual cities and virtual worlds. The cutting edge of urban modelling now represents populations as individual agents whose movement within the city is the focus. In a sense, when we embed ourselves in virtual environments, we move as we navigate, generating real behaviour in a virtual space. Building mathematical models of what we see and how we move involves a reverse symmetry based on simulated behaviour in a virtual space, and such possibilities are only just beginning to be realised. Figure 10 shows how we embed such models into digital space and visualise their form, not only in 2-D, but also in 3-D.

In London, we are hard at work building models of local movement, of the way pedestrians move through the city, and the decisions that motivate their movement. We have built agent-based models of the Notting Hill Carnival – a highly stage-managed event that is heavily controlled yet subject to a variety of public-safety problems. We have also begun work on models of flows in dense entertainment areas of the city such as Covent Garden, focusing on modelling how visitors negotiate this space. These are not avatars, but agents, in that our aim is to replicate real behaviours and then embed these within the virtual scene, visualising agents in 3-D and getting them to move through the virtual city. Our progress is shown in Figure 10, which contrasts real crowds with a simulated variety.

The environments we can create thus contain 3-D digital cities of the conventional kind, like Virtual London, populated with abstract numerical data, interspersed with multimedia such as photorealistic panoramas. These can be accessible to other web sites from within the scene, into which real-time 'live' data might be fed. These digital, yet nevertheless conventional, environments might then be imported into virtual worlds in which we, as avatars, enter the scene, moving among the digital forms, experiencing each other 'remotely', and thus being subjected to the real-time data feeds from the real city. Mathematical models of such real-time data can be instantaneously created and agents generated to interweave and intersperse with ourselves – the avatars.

Such environments are almost there, revealing enormous possibilities for innovative and exciting ways in which we might think about design and planning and the management of change. More importantly, these parallel worlds open up the design of our cities to a much wider public, as well as transforming the way we might deliver services, seek information and engage in new kinds of dialogue. The positive side of such virtualities implies a richness that intimately reflects the real world and should, with care, enhance it. ᴆ

Notes
1 Jean Baudrillard, *Simulacra and Simulation*, University of Michigan Press (Ann Arbor, MI), 1994.
2 LIDAR: light imaging detection and radar.

Acknowledgements
The authors wish to thank the Greater London Authority, Ordnance Survey, Infoterra and ESRI for their support in the projects quoted herein. Steve Evans was central to the development of the Virtual London 3-D-GIS and CAD models reported here.

A Vertical Public Space. The Dreaming Wall is a project for a blank wall in a historical square of Milan, and was originally submitted for a competition promoted by Diesel. It was conceived as an info-forum. A vertical public space reflecting the dual character of the city, it has a double life, just as the city and the piazza do – white and subdued during the day, glowing phosphorescent green at night.

Collective Subconscious. The wall is seen as a tool of cultural, simultaneous and random collective communication, creating a visual buzz. As a public digital billboard, at night its surface randomly displays text messages sent by people standing in the square, or from anywhere else in the world via the Internet. The messages are generated in real time by a chemical reaction between a computer-controlled UV laser projection and phosphorescent panels on the wall, which are 'excited' by the UV light and so release the glowing text. Messages last 15 minutes before being reabsorbed by the wall. This constant transience metaphorically suggests the subconsciousness of a city asleep.

www.conceptualdevices.com/ENG/dreamingwall/index.html

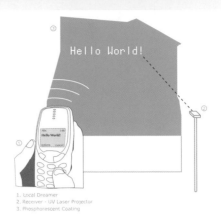

1. Local Dreamer
2. Receiver – UV Laser Projector
3. Phosphorescent Coating

A Scarponi, S Massa, F Pedrini and B Galassi, Dreaming Wall info-forum project, Milan, Italy, 2004
Diagram of the interaction system between text messages sent by people and the Dreaming Wall's glowing surface. A computer-controlled UV laser projector collects the messages and writes them on the wall surface, 'exciting' its panels with a chemical reaction generated by UV light, which releases a glowing text on the wall.

A daylight view of the Dreaming Wall, when its photophorescent panels are 'uncharged',

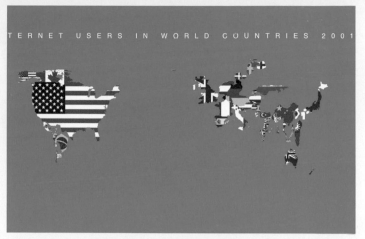

Antonio Scarponi, Population in World Countries, 2002
Population in World Countries is part of a project called Human World, an atlas that represents the world from the point of view of its population. This map, or cartogram, shows the area of each state proportional to its population: 1 pixel = 1,000 people.

Antonio Scarponi, Internet Users in World Countries, 2002
Internet Users in World Countries is also part of the Human World project. This map shows the area of each state proportionally to people connected to the Internet: 1 pixel = 1,000 people.

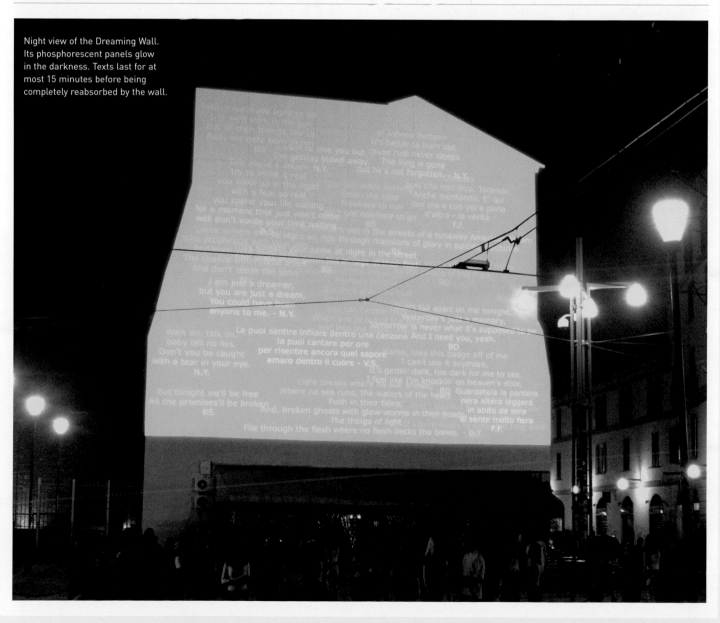

Night view of the Dreaming Wall. Its phosphorescent panels glow in the darkness. Texts last for at most 15 minutes before being completely reabsorbed by the wall.

THE 21ST-CENTURY WELFARE CITY:

AALBORG + COPENHAGEN, DENMARK

Under the scientific eye of satellite surveillance, the world's urban conglomerations often appear heterogeneous. On the ground, differences and special features of a city remain of utmost importance to the quality of life of its citizens. **Hans Kiib** and **Gitte Marling** assess how the welfare system in Denmark, which is so dear to many Danes, is holding up. If the physical, Modernist urban model of the welfare city is to endure, can it withstand the irresistible, less tangible pull of consumption and aspirational individualised lifestyles that are penetrating the globe worldwide?

Coop Himmelb(l)au, Aalborg House of Music, Denmark, 2005
Aalborg harbour front is part of a huge urban redevelopment and cultural planning strategy. The House of Music is to be an integrated co-location of the Symphonic Orchestra, dance companies, experimental theatre, undergraduate and masters programmes in music, music therapy, design, urban design, architecture and multimedia. Furthermore, it will be followed by a range of cultural incubators for small firms and shops. The partners are a mix of private and public institutions including private investors, regional municipalities, ministries, the local university and educational institutions.

Reidum takes her bike to the large suburban shopping mall to buy some groceries and clothes for her youngest daughter. It is hard to find her way between the parked cars, but she does not complain. This is her everyday domain, and here she feels safe – here she can buy everything she needs.

At the mall, a group of architecture students are exhibiting design proposals for the whole area. Some of the projects clearly take their inspiration from high-rise Asian architecture, but most relate to typical Nordic architecture – lots of glass. One of the students speaks English on a mobile phone, and two of the girls are clearly not from Denmark.

In Copenhagen, the new metro between the city centre and the airport passes by. Although most people now use it for commuting, the metro is also bridging the gap between the city and the larger world. Businesspeople, backpackers and elderly citizens taking a holiday in the sun pass by in a multicoloured stream of people, suitcases and newspapers of different nationalities. At the same time, large screens in the mall displaying commercials and 24-hour news reports link suburban living with global adventures and catastrophes, reminding us that we are all part of it.

Reidum returns to her 109-square-metre apartment in a nice low, yet dense, neighbourhood. Her two children are playing in front of the house. Her husband is unemployed and she is attending an educational programme at the technical college during the day. Reidum and her family are supported by the public welfare system, which provides them with money and social housing. But some day she will earn her own living. Just 15 minutes' walk from her home she has an allotment garden with a small cottage. This is where the family spend their spare time during spring and summer; all of their hopes and dreams are connected to this place.

This narrative of suburban living is influenced by at least two global transformation processes. First, increased mobility and the agglomeration of towns and landscape into meta-urban fields, including a network urbanisation of towns, suburbs and landscape related to the infrastructural development.[1] Second, a transition from industry – and service-based economies – to a global knowledge-based economy,[2] or experience economy.[3]

Focusing on 21st-century living in Scandinavia, this development raises a number of questions, some of which will be addressed here. What is the impact of meta-urbanisation on Danish towns and postwar welfare living? In what way will different areas of the city be transformed? How will the experience economy influence city life and the spatial distribution of functions and programmes? And how will increased mobility and individual control of time and space influence different lifestyles and ways of experiencing the new urban field?[4]

The story of the Danish welfare state is important to the Danes, as it has become a part of their national identity. It is a fundamental, core story about equal rights in the broadest sense of the term, which was originally told in order to break the class divisions and gender roles of the industrial society. The welfare paradigm is linked to equal access to the consumption of goods, education, housing and social services. The concept also includes access to

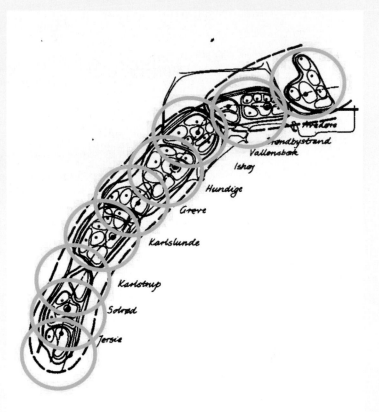

Danish planning tradition

In the 1950s, an overall ribbon-band city model was developed in the Copenhagen region, the so-called 'Finger Plan'. As a part of this plan, the 'Køge Bugt Plan' was implemented along the southern finger of Copenhagen. The Køge Bugt Plan represented the functionalist approach to the welfare state *par excellence,* with its public infrastructure and location of public and private service facilities close to the railway stations, forming a row of neighbourhoods. Other elements included the public housing programme and landscape projects, including a new beach park along the coast. By the 1960s, the aesthetic of many of the housing projects was high-rise functional minimalism – an architectural representation far from traditional Danish architecture. Even though such projects had many welfare benefits, they were soon abandoned and replaced with new schemes of low and dense housing projects and single-family houses.

Songlines

Reidum (age 32) belongs to the low-income group, and her family is supported by the public welfare system. Her suburban domain is mostly determined by accessibility by bike or on foot. We use the term 'songlines' to describe the domains, or urban territories, of individuals. People weave their own city experiences and townscapes by means of local and international songlines.[5] Their songlines differ quantitatively and qualitatively – differences determined by the individual's home and residential district, financial situation and lifestyle. However, the songlines of rich and middle-class Danes are extending to include areas with summer cottages (house number two) and holiday destinations outside the boundaries of the country.

Reidum's home, Aalborg, Denmark
Reidum and her family are living in a low-rise social housing apartment. The social housing programme had its starting point in the 19th century and now covers a third of all city homes.

Five decades after the welfare project was launched, it seems to have worked. From a structural perspective, the urban model has proved to be a robust concept that has survived changing economic and political circumstances.

Reidum's allotment garden, Aalborg, Denmark
The first Danish allotment garden was established in Aalborg in 1884 as a result of a Labour Party policy. The goal was to provide Danish working-class families with a piece of land within cycling distance of their homes in the city. Here, the families were able to build a small cottage, to grow vegetables for their own consumption, and to relax in green surroundings. These settlements are still very popular. Today, they are particularly attractive to young families as a supplement to a flat. The cottages become larger, more luxurious and with the facilities of a summer house. The allotment gardens are an important part of the Danish welfare city's identity, and some have been declared national heritages.

employment and to democratic and political resources. Various policies and institutions have been linked to these concepts; for example, matters concerning location and distribution of urban centres, land-use regulation, urban renewal and public housing.[6]

Urban planning and design have been important tools in implementing welfare policies. Every sector and every piece of land in the country has been discussed, planned and regulated. The development of Denmark's welfare city in the 20th century was based on a combination of two basic planning models: the ribbon-band city model focusing on accessibility and distribution of goods, services and education; and the so-called urban-neighbourhood city model, focusing on the hierarchy of centres, community planning and participation in the formulation of developmental goals.[7] This vision of the welfare city thus combines a modernistic idea of a rational urban machine, ensuring the appropriate location of urban functions in an effective web of access structures, with a preindustrial organisational principle of neighbourhood units and communities.

Five decades after the welfare project was launched, it seems to have worked. From a structural perspective, the urban model has proved to be a robust concept that has survived changing economic and political circumstances.[8] The transport system is efficient: mobility is ensured and access to consumer goods and electronic media is overwhelming. The standard of housing is high for everybody, and there is a wide range of housing and many types of ownership.[9] Furthermore, vast numbers of women have entered the labour market, and the explosion in education is tremendous.

However, increased mobility has undermined the reality of existing local communities. The mental image of the welfare city is increasingly becoming an incoherent phenomenon based on individualised patterns of dwelling and consumption behaviour. Aesthetic preferences are no longer manifested in a strong neighbourhood identity. Instead, they appear as a pattern of the individualised use of city services, means of transport, leisure habits, meetings, shopping and other issues. It could even be said that some of the ideals of equality and homogeneity have been supplemented by ideals of difference and diversity at the individual level.[10]

Welfare-City Experiments

The decline of polluting industry and the rise of postindustrial service industries have made space for cleaner technologies and a strong focus on environmental issues. Over the past decades, so-called 'urban ecology' has been promoted as Denmark's official policy. Massive investment in waste and wastewater treatment, and in sustainable energy supplies, has resulted in a better environment in general, and has also created new possibilities for city life. Furthermore, a range of more local social experiments in urban ecology, involving the users and local partners, has taken place, including public-supported urban-renewal and eco-building experiments. Such projects are now springing up all over the country.

Urban renewal and urban policy are main programmes of the welfare city. Suggestions for public investments and

planning strategies have been followed up by private initiatives and, as a result, old city centres, including the old working-class settlements and the more modern settlements from the 1960s, have been renewed.

Today, the traditional housing-oriented urban-renewal programme is combined with social programmes that provide local meeting places for cultural exchange, sports and education. This has made the centres of nearly all of Denmark's cities highly attractive, not only to those who cannot afford a villa, but also for students and young people (known as DINKS = double income no kids), who prefer to live in the city centres adjacent to the cultural zones. In addition, there is a steady flow of elderly people (aged 60+), who are moving from their suburban villas into flats in the city centres. Thus, Denmark's city centres have become a social mix of different cultures, including some newly arrived from elsewhere in the world. In subsequent years, such development will be supported by the refocusing of city programmes towards cultural events and institutions.

Cultural Field Operation

Presumably, Denmark's new investment in, and policies for, its city centres will extend their power. Former working-class neighbourhoods will become self-

Sustainable infrastructure, Copenhagen, Denmark
In Copenhagen, the new metro projects have led to an increase in internal city mobility. The metro enables the relocation of enterprises and other transport-generating functions close to railway stations, which is followed by public and private investments in urban renewal.

PLOT, Copenhagen Harbour Bath, Copenhagen, Denmark, 2003
Over a decade the municipality has increased water quality via strong regulations and wastewater treatment. Today the results are evident with new leisure activities on the harbour fronts of all Danish cities, strengthening the quality of urban life and creating new kinds of social meetings in public spaces.

propagated Latin quarters and bohemian milieus. Harbour fronts will be rejuvenated, and new cultural investment parks will emerge in a corporate symbiosis, with educational establishments and public domains related to urban events and lifestyles.

The city centres are an important part of Danish city branding. Their historic buildings, pedestrian streets, small squares and parks make them perfect bases for large-scale cultural and sporting events, which are often used to brand cities in their struggle for a favourable position in the new cultural urbanisation. Such concentrations of entertainment, culture and recreation within, or close to historical city centres strengthen the role of 'the public meeting place of the welfare city'. The content of these historical hearts is changing towards exposure and amusement, yet also towards social and cultural exchange.

Urban Infra-Field Development

High-speed road and rail networks reduce the temporal distance between cities. At the regional level, the 'one-hour-city', defined by its accessibility by car or train within

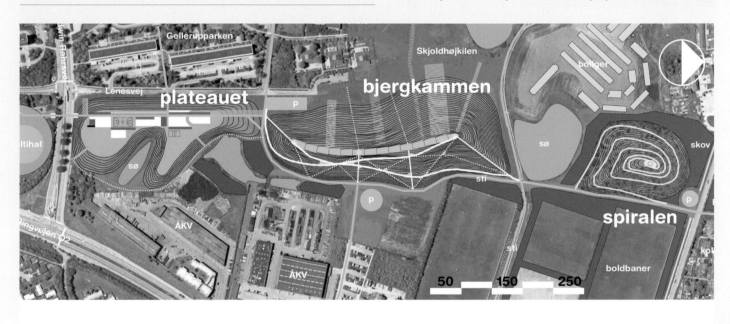

Transform – Architects, Hasle Hills, Århus, Denmark, 2004
Treatment and reuse of earth left over from building activities in the city. The previously problematic piles of earth have been transformed into new public meeting places where the activities of different cultures and lifestyles are combined.

an hour, is now covering a much larger area than it did 20 years ago, and the Danish H-infra-city model from the early 1960s, which links a range of towns and suburbs into bands of urban fields, appears to be more relevant than ever. The H-infra-city model included all larger cities linked together with freeways and high-speed trains. The distinction between 'city' and 'landscape' will be increasingly blurred as the cityscape and the landscape are layered and merged into the 'urban infra-field'. Nevertheless, development along the infrastructure is not dominated by an increase in population. Urban extension is based on larger houses or by doubling the number of houses per family unit. Furthermore, new landscapes related to former industrial zones or former agricultural

Cultural Bazar, Islands Brygge, Copenhagen, Denmark
In many cases, the transformation of harbour fronts is related to restaurants and high-end cultural tourism. However, in others it is community based and related to a social strategy focusing on cultural exchange and mixed experiences. In summer, several generations and different ethnic groups occupy the harbour-front staircase during the day and at night, enjoying each other's company and the flowing water.

Welfare policy is a priority of all Denmark's political parties. It is currently a combination of traditional policies on social security and a packet of new policies on urban ecology, urban physics, cultural planning and cultural exchange.

landscapes will emerge inside the city, or as surplus land related to new infrastructures between cities.[11] Such development provides a 'new countryside zone', transformable to domains for low, dense housing programmes, summer cottages or allotment gardens. Summer cottages along the coastline are developing into large countryside suburbias for the rich, and more and more people are looking for allotment cottages in more remote parts of the surplus landscape.

Sensing the Future Welfare City

Mobility and globalisation have a strong impact on the welfare city, although it appears to be both stable and suited for the new trends. The welfare programmes do not seem to be overruled, as welfare policy is a priority of all Denmark's political parties. It is currently a combination of traditional policies on social security and a packet of new policies on urban ecology, urban physics, cultural planning and cultural exchange.

However, the dissolution of the stable territorial city with permanent functions into the network city requires new interpretations of the concepts of building, dwelling and living. Because of this, and because of the multi-ethnic and multicultural development of Danish society, the fundamental core story of the welfare city has to be rewritten in order to make it more inclusive and open to change. 'Flexicurity' is the key word in this strategy. The open Danish society has turned out to be both safe and flexible. Social security and free education combined with accessibility and public housing programmes have provided the fundamental basis for all inhabitants to develop their skills and enhance their knowledge without economic or social risk. This means that the labour market is very flexible and attractive to knowledge-based international organisations.

It could be argued that this model, in many ways, should be a role model for many countries who are in search of alternative models to that of a neoliberal market-driven development. It is possible to learn a lot from more than 50 years of Scandinavian welfare-city development, but it takes commitment to the general idea behind the model – including equality, openness and high taxes. ∆

Notes
1 Manuel Castells, *The Information Age: Economy, Society and Culture*, Blackwell (Oxford), 2003. Stephen Graham and Simon Marvin, *Splintering Urbanism*, Routledge (London and New York), 2002.
2 Bob Jessob, 'Recent societal and urban change', in Tom Nielsen, Niels Albertsen and Peter Hemmersham (eds), *Urban Mutation*, Arkitektskolens Forlag (Denmark), 2004.
3 Joseph B Pine and James H Gillmore, *The Experience Economy*, Harvard Business School Press (Boston, MA), 1999.
4 These questions have also been raised in the USE project coordinated by S Boeri. See S Boeri, 'USE: Uncertain States of Europe', in S Boeri, S Kwinter, N Tazi and HU Obrist, *Mutations*, Actar (Barcelona), 2000.
5 Gitte Marling, *Urban Songlines*, Aalborg University Press (Denmark), 2003.
6 A Gårdmand, *Dansk byplanlægning 1938–1992* (Urban Planning in Denmark, 1938–1992), Arkitektens Forlag (Copenhagen),1993.
7 Hans Kiib, 'The consumption landscape of the welfare city', in Claus Bech-Danielsen, Ole Michael Jensen, Hans Kiib and Gitte Marling, *Urban Lifescape – Space, Lifestyle, Consumption*, Aalborg University Press (Denmark), 2004.
8 *Ibid.*
9 Thorkild Ærø, 'The housing project of Denmark's welfare society: ideals and needs related to housing', in Bech-Danielsen, Jensen, Kiib and Marling, *op cit*.
10 Gitte Marling, 'Urban songlines: the space of daily life in the city', in Bech-Danielsen, Jensen, Kiib and Marling, *op cit*.
11 Tom Nielsen and Peter Hemmersam, 'Imagine the H-City: Denmark as an urban field', in Nielsen, Albertsen and Hemmersam (eds), *op cit*.

City of Wilderness – Rethinking the European Città Diffusa: French/Belgian Border

As the EU strengthens its global identity and at the same time expands its territory, its internal boundaries are transforming and allowing a new type of urban environment to emerge in areas that formerly resisted being fixed by national borders. These unclaimed 'a-territories', where landscapes intertwine with borders, provide the space to rethink the traditional relationship between city and nature: a new kind of wilderness.

Most of the words we use to describe a wilderness – 'void', 'uninhabitable', 'uncontrolled' – represent something other than human, a world of beasts and gods, a space that ranges from hell to heaven. With the disappearance of borders in the EU, a new wilderness has appeared, a new kind of transnational space that does not distinguish human production from natural processes.

A closer look at Flanders Fields, where mirror towns have developed on both sides of the French/Belgian border, reveals border pockets of unclaimed space, potential zones for a supranational city. Here, the new city of wilderness could tie together international territories on the grounds of a common landscape. This offers the potential to reconnect the forgotten essence of untamed nature in borderlands to their human inhabitation, as a new urban model – the city of wilderness.

VIRTUAL WEB SPACE

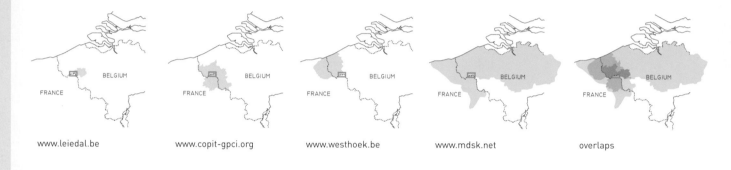

www.leiedal.be   www.copit-gpci.org   www.westhoek.be   www.mdsk.net   overlaps

TRANSPORT NETWORKS

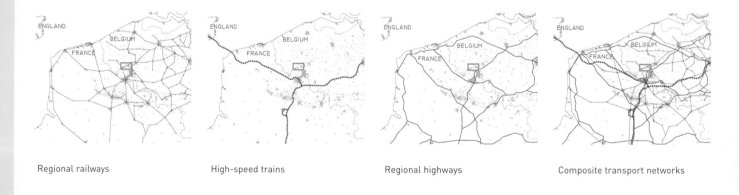

Regional railways   High-speed trains   Regional highways   Composite transport networks

TERRITORIAL PATCHES

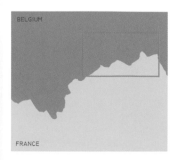
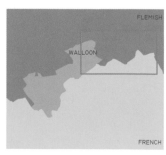

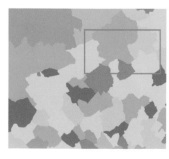

National patches   Language patches   Department/arrondissement patches   Commune patches

SUPRANATIONAL SPACE

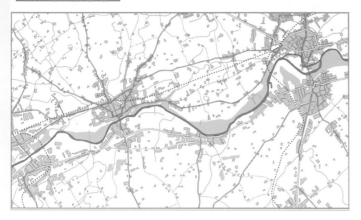

1960: Mirror cities have developed along the border, which still coincides with the river.

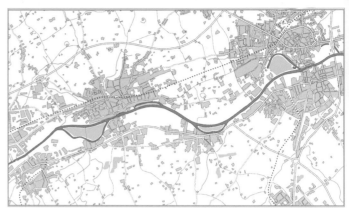

Current: Cities are melting together across the border, the former wilderness has been tamed and the river has been straightened.

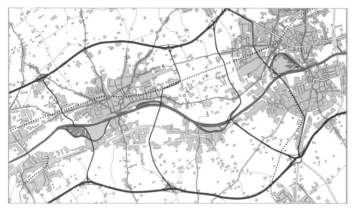

+5 years: The islands created between the new course of the river and the border offer opportunities for reinserting the 'wild', connected by a supranational transport-networked landscape.

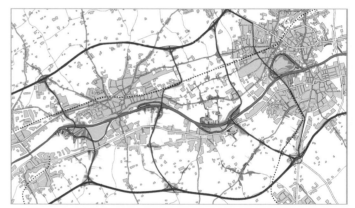

+15 years: A future 'city of new wilderness' can grow from these transformations in a postnational condition where built and natural space have merged.

ISLAND INSERTION

Whereas wilderness has been traditionally linked to nonhuman nature (first nature), the new wilderness can include humans and human production (second nature). A new balance between first and second natures becomes a tool for envisioning the supranational space of future EU territory.

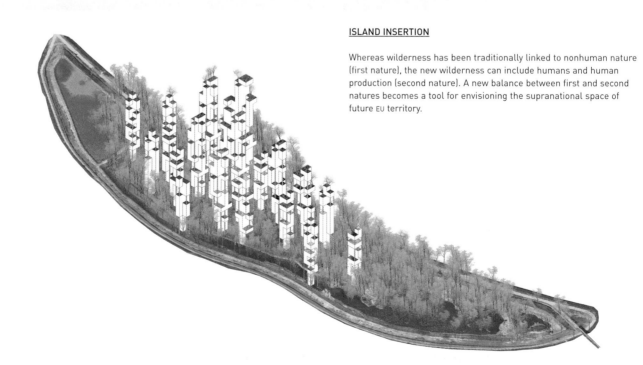

SQUATTING GEOMETRIES
– GUERILLA BARCELONA:
TECHNOLOGICAL APPROPRIATIONS OF THE OVER– PLANNED CITY

Technological gap
19th-century telecommunications vs Jean Nouvel's
AGBAR Tower, Barcelona, 2005.

All space is already occupied by the enemy, which has even reshaped its elementary laws, its geometry, to its own purposes.
— Attila Kotányi and Raoul Vaneigem, 1961[1]

PART 1
Architecture after Barcelona
Barcelona exemplifies better than any other global city the mix-ups of Postmodern city planning. It has intelligently responded to the characteristic decentralisation of the 1970s, and since the early 1990s has exemplified a skilful urban renewal. The jump to the global stage as a cultural metropolis of leisure and well-being marks a transition from a functional city model towards a city understood as the locus of the conspicuous display of accumulation of resources, and as a mediated image of cosmopolitan life.

This transition can actually be seen as the corruption of a socially oriented model satisfying collective interests into one by which private interests, mostly related to real estate aided by public institutions, are taking control of the urban-renewal process.

Simultaneously, new citizen associations join forces in order to promote urban transformations at a local level, or to oppose decisions taken by the city authorities. A new urban subjectivity appears. New parameters in the reformulation of a collective history can be defined within the gap between city and individual.

Technological Subjectivity
Today, new subversive subjectivities are framing collective life in different ways than was the case in the city's shopping malls, bars and markets at the beginning of the 1990s.

These subjectivities are characterised by the reconciliation of individuals with urban space by means of technology. No longer do citizens pursue the reproduction of the postindustrial city's collective form; instead they deploy the urgency of a latent collective desire. In doing this, through portable communication and remote-sensing technologies, they are transforming the use and perception of the city. Instantaneous, just-in-time experience constitutes a heightening of the present moment rather than a historical recollection of time and space.

In Barcelona, in a radically subversive way, this takes the form of civil disobedience, technological guerrilla activities, GPS-guided *dérive* or Temporary Autonomous Zones.[2]

In the 1980s, Barcelona became the darling of urban regeneration. Its mayor and city authorities gained awards and recognition the world over. However, 111 architects José Luis Echeverría Manau, Jordi Mansilla Ortoneda and Jorge Perea Solano depict a very different, more sinister view of the city's development, in which the metropolis has been reshaped to serve private rather than civic interests. They explain how subversive citizens' groups are hitting back and realising their collective power through the strategic, yet often spontaneous use of portable communication and remote-sensing technologies.

Public space has shifted from acting as a strategic catalyst to become an overdesigned showcase of the city. The recovery and reoccupation of the historical centre during the early 1990s is being counteracted by massive migrations of industry and urban youth to the city's second and third peripheries. Finally, the construction of high-rise corporate-like gated communities such as Diagonal Mar is overriding the urgency for new public space and housing typologies.

The main consequence of this 'evolved' transformation model, made possible through the pervasive manipulation of the idea of public realm, is the deep disjuncture between city form and citizenship.

Today, the city inhabitant is conscious of being, or having been, instrumentalised as an actor of a supposed social agreement in favour of the city's continuous state of transformation. The consequential distrust towards public institutions is leading to the strengthening of civic associations and the appearance of filo-anarchist social constructs, such as cyberpunk and squatter collectives, and local anarchist activism.

Citizens claim individuality beyond possible classifications of class and gender, as the ever more diverse and fragmented supply of leisure and commerce makes it more difficult to define and fix collective-use patterns in the city.

Global underground scene
Barcelona and New York show tags (artists' painted logos) designed in ... Tokyo?

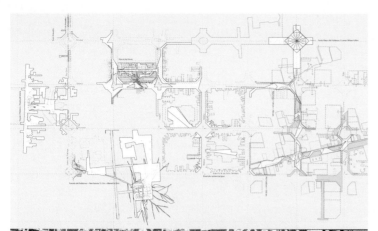

Event representation vs figure-ground
111's experiential map of the Idefons Cerdà grid, 1859 (top) and
Giambattista Nolli's map of Rome, 1748 (bottom).

New technologies play a key
role in reorganising the use
of streets, corners, stations
and bars, redefining their value
in the urban collective realm

The spontaneous demonstrations that occurred in Barcelona after the 11 March 2004 terrorist attacks in Madrid made people aware for the first time of the enormous impact of portable telecommunications technologies on our society. In a matter of hours, thousands of people were summoned via SMS (mobile-phone text messaging) to join together in a demonstration to demand political responsibility from the Spanish government.

Such horizontal communication tactics are also the basis of social disobedience actions such as Practica kittin', an initiative that emerged in the Gràcia district of Barcelona. An informal practice of removing the commercial posters of speculators from walls, cars and other elements of the urban environment was systematised across the district via email, generating a virtual community against real-estate speculative processes.

Using similar communication protocols, 'book-crossers' around the world share books by leaving them around the city (benches, bus stops, bar tables and public toilets) and simultaneously revealing to the local book-crosser community the book's precise location, thus reformulating the idea of sharing, while generating communities bound by Internet forums.

This new urban phenomenology, also related to remote-sensing technologies like GPS or GIS, is specific to the technological character of this new subjectivity and its impact on mobility and the mechanisms through which humans relate to an urban framework. The innovation lies in the capacity to connect forms of virtual community with physical proximities and collective construction.

It is necessary to emphasise the subversive value of such technologies against the urban allocation of uses and codes to the built space, both public and private. New technologies play a key role in reorganising the use of streets, corners, stations and bars, redefining their value in the urban collective realm. Technological subversion allows individuals to specialise and spatialise their differences and decide their affiliations: mobility and individualism converge.

The new virtual nature of the city – City of Flows, City of Bits, Informational City – mostly theorised by geographers and sociologists, has led to a situation whereby the city is

Summon digitally, act physically
Guerrilla communication tactics in Barcelona.

111 architects, urban proposal for downtown Valencia, Spain, 2004
The bands sweeping across the area provide the geometrical base for built
interventions and unplanned events. Bandwidth dimension, based on
structural standards, cannot anticipate the desired programmes to be
developed in the area.

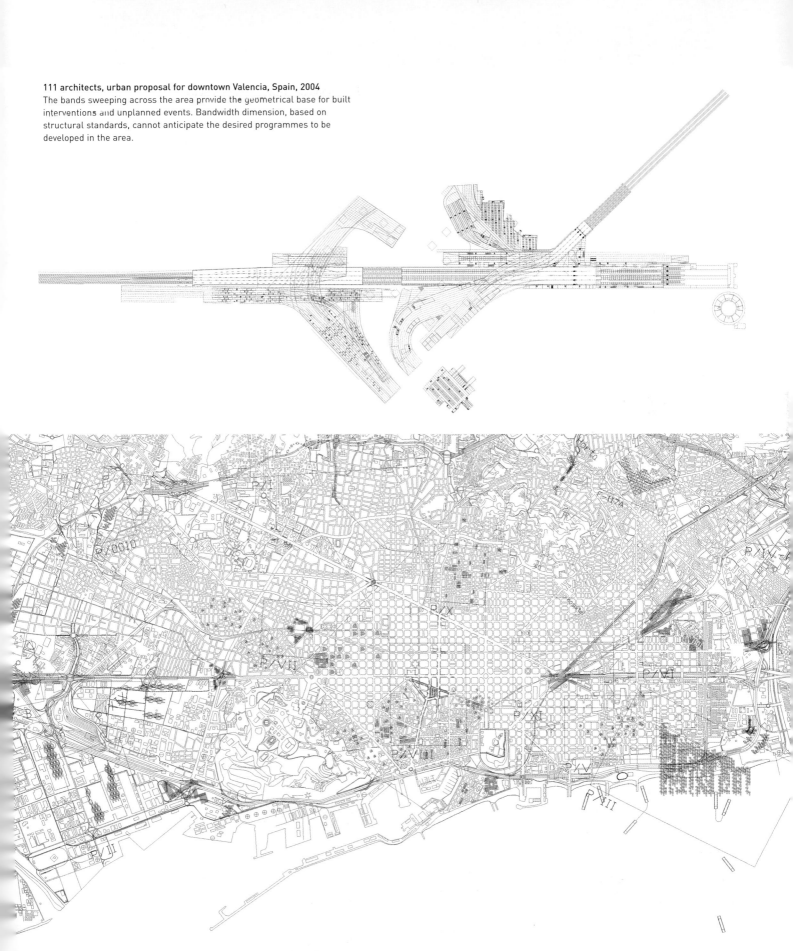

111 architects, mapping of Barcelona's master plan strategic locations, 2005
The mapping shows the strategic locations taken over by squatting
geometries as a means of providing new opportunities for interventions
within overdesigned and overcontrolled city areas.

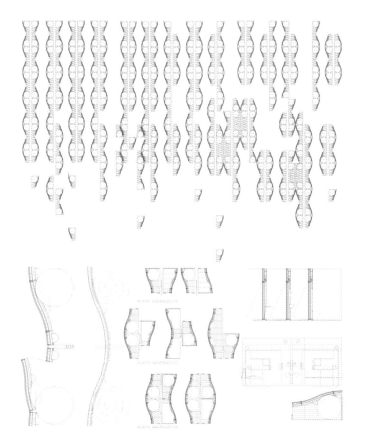

111 architects, urban shelter for Toyo Ito's 'Nomad Women', 2004
As a homage to Ito's Dwelling for the Tokyo Nomad Women (1985), the urban shelter is a surface that, when attached to existing urban structures, provides a space for beauty care, relaxation and information.

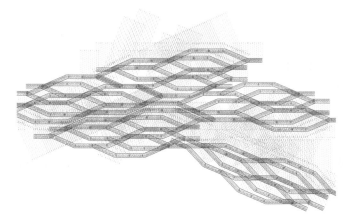

111 architects, megastructure for 150,000 people in Amposta, Spain, 2004
A rigid, repetitive, standardised, neutral 'hardware' shell provides for flexible, exceptional, specialised infill as the activating 'software'.

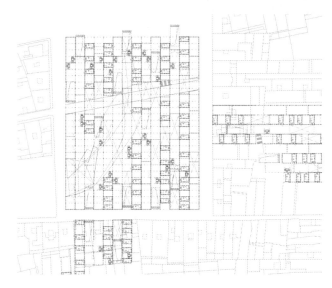

111 architects, housing replacement plan in El Raval of Barcelona, Spain, 2004
18th-century housing replacement project based on the understanding of its geometrical constraints: structural span and maximum depth.

theorised as a virtual construct, often disregarding its physical dimension. Since the figure-ground relation that validated the understanding of the urban fabric prior to the 19th-century industrial city is no longer valid, new tools, methodologies, design and planning figures should be provided in order to analyse, and intervene within, the complexity of the contemporary urban environment.

The second part of this article looks at the specificity and power of geometry as a transforming agent from the perspective of architecture and urban design, and calls for a revision and updating of geometry-based methodologies that are capable of dealing with present urban conditions.

PART 2
The Unstable Figure: Unstable Ground Duality and the Geometric Interface

The concepts of unstable figure and unstable ground should help in recovering the physicality, measurability and geometrical relations of the city that much of recent urban theory has failed to take into account. At the same time, this physicality should be considered from the perspective of the unstable spatialisation that characterises many contemporary cities.

In our context, the unstable ground embodies both figure and ground (built and nonbuilt) as a collapsed 3-D whole, whereas the unstable figure comprehends population, economic and informational dynamics.

In the case of Barcelona, the unstable ground is affected simultaneously by the need for permanent morphological transformation (to fulfil the demands of the real-estate market and

construction industry), and by permanent programmatic reinvention that satisfies an ever more demanding local consumer and the tourism economy. In parallel, the instability of the figure becomes a direct consequence, not only of the summation and collision of individual trajectories within the city, but also of the impact of portable communication technologies on these individual agents, enabling hyper-connectivity, real-time decision making and panoptical control.

The origin of the geometric interface (GI) lies in the necessity to manage the constant misalignment of unstable figure and unstable ground. As in software, its value resides in its capacity to articulate feedback processes between environment and user. It operates as a negotiatiating tool that manages use, shape and emergent appropriation of space. The interface not only deals with the tension between unstable figure and unstable ground that is common to the physical and programmatic evolution of the city in relation to its inhabitants, but also organises the necessary interaction between space and citizen to

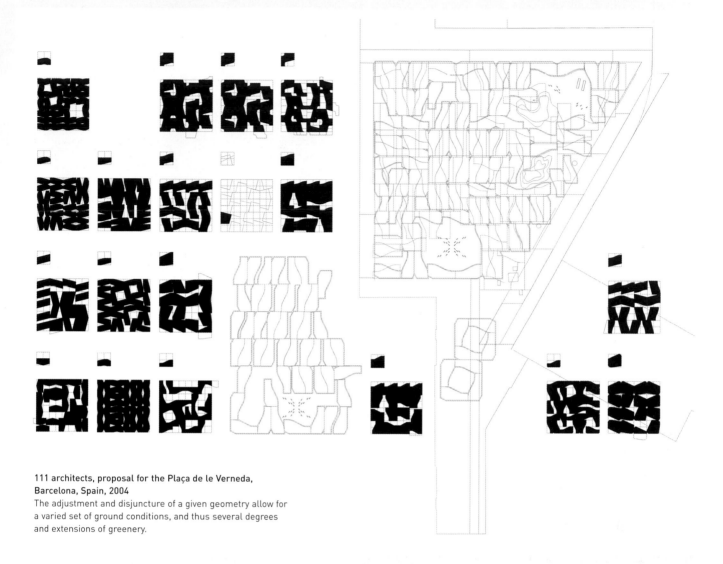

111 architects, proposal for the Plaça de le Verneda,
Barcelona, Spain, 2004
The adjustment and disjuncture of a given geometry allow for
a varied set of ground conditions, and thus several degrees
and extensions of greenery.

evolve collectively. The GI appears as a qualitative step in
the joint figure-ground of urban contexts.

Geometric interface is the name given to the beta version
of an early intuition: a new category of planning/urban design
figure that transcends the oversimplifying top-down approach
of the master plan, as well as the inoperative abstraction of
the bottom-up urban-design strategy. Instead, it operates
through predefined 3-D thresholds related to various levels
of physical intensity (building code, infrared, soundwave,
collective mind, digital cable, vegetation, soft
infrastructure, building, hard infrastructure and so on).

Acknowledging that urban design always relates to a
physical, measurable, built reality (whether it is about
paving streets, information technologies and
communicaton (ITC) infrastructure or urban policy), the GI
calls for a renewed faith in geometry – informed geometry,
strategic geometry – as a transforming agent. Distance and
size are GI's main tactical parameters from which any other
consideration (possible uses, possible densities, possible
occupancies, possible floor area rations) will evolve.

The GI could be promoted by an urban-planning agency or
as a private planning initiative, but should be 'used' through
a nonplanned, noncentralised and nonregulated collective
act of appropriation developed over time. Squatting is the
ultimate purpose of the geometric interface.

CONCLUSION
Squatting Geometries
In 1997, the editorial of the *Architecture after Geometry* issue of
Δ stated that: 'Geometry's role has been to provide the armature
of substantiation for architecture ...'.[3] We hardly understand what
this editorial is about. We think our time calls for a different
understanding of things. We are not fascinated by the mystics of
geometry or technology either; we just want to know how to use
them. For us, using means understanding.

Nowadays, communication and remote-sensing technologies are
incorporated in daily life in a natural and even absent-minded way.
As architects, we must understand that through technology almost
every citizen has evolved into a new type of urbanising agent,
creating an opportunity for new forms of urbanity and urbanism. Our
role is to design, from the specificity of our discipline, the geometric
frame that guarantees the organised yet free action of such agents:
a sort of open-source urbanism through which intelligent, ethical
and truly democratic postglobal cities are possible. Δ

Notes
1 Attila Kotànyi and Raoul Vaneigem, 'Programme élémentaire du Bureau d'urbanisme
unitaire' (Basic programme for the Office of Unitary Urbanism', *Internationale
situationniste*, No 6, August 1961.
2 Hakim Bay, *The Temporary Autonomous Zone, Ontological Anarchy, Poetic
Terrorism*, Autonomedia Anti-copyright (New York), 1985.
3 Peter Davidson and Donald Bates, Editorial, Δ Profile No 127, 1998.

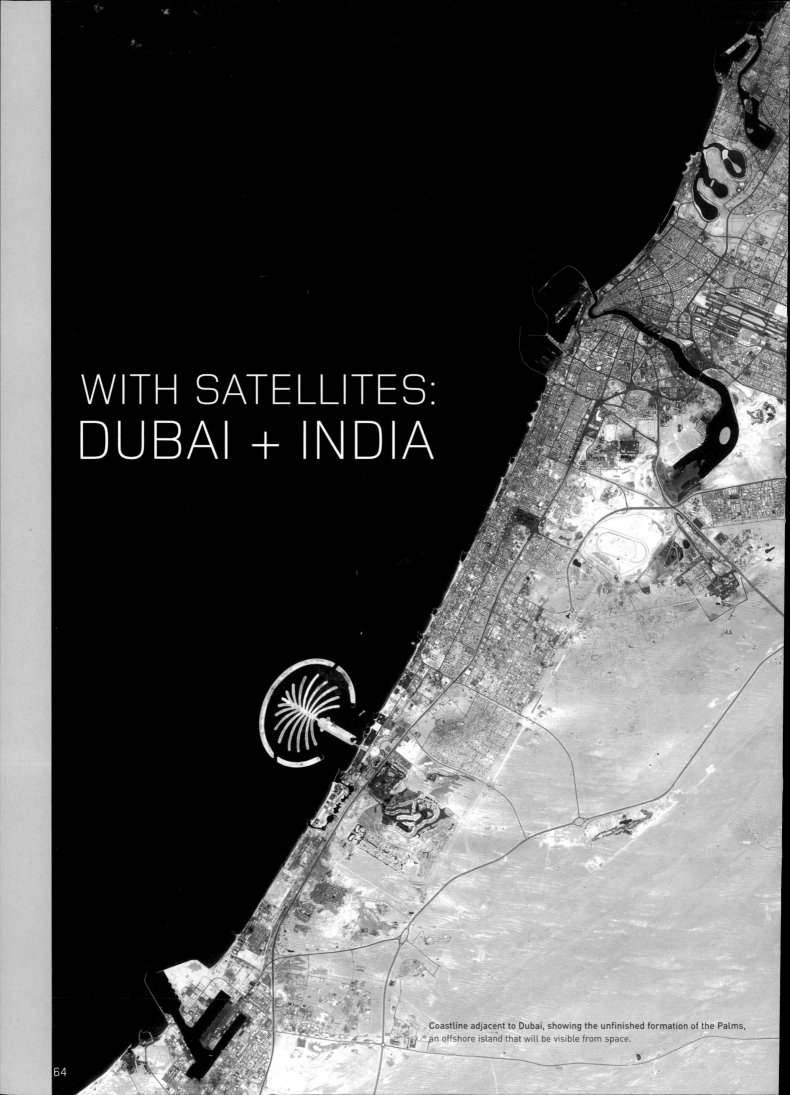

WITH SATELLITES:
DUBAI + INDIA

Coastline adjacent to Dubai, showing the unfinished formation of the Palms, an offshore island that will be visible from space.

Satellites named *Optus*, *Telstar*, *Eurobird*, *Hot Bird* or *Atlantic Bird* beam down overlapping spots of microwaves to the receiving territories below, transmitting Zee TV, STAR TV and Al Jazeera to Abu Dhabi, Mumbai or Singapore.[1] These supposed instruments of the fabled global village have produced not a single global village, but a number of global villages. National and commercial consortiums stratify the microwave sea of transmissions, making it increasingly more dense, codified and politicised.

While developed countries with military or space-race technologies established the first satellite consortium, or village, developing countries subsequently established their own fleets or villages. Arthur C Clarke's *Extra-Terrestrial Relays* (1945), a scenario about the potential power of global satellite TV, was perhaps first tested with NASA's

tone favoured by futurology, Toffler called for an agrarian democracy, a Gandhian pastoral or rural village served by satellite communication.[5] Indeed, while most satellite fleets have some defence or military intelligence capability, many of the satellite villages or neighbourhoods initially used them for nation building and resource management.

In India, the often-published portrait of Vikram Sarabhai presides over a pool of microwaves that initially possessed this political disposition. Looking beatifically skyward as the father of the Indian space programme, Sarabhai, an adviser to Indira Gandhi and a mascot of sorts for Toffler's satellite projections, hoped to combine high technology with the dream of a rural broadcast. This airborne infrastructure was to reinforce a Gandhian or Nehruvian political ethos, like dams on a microwave sea. The India Space Resource Organization (ISRO) was established

By juxtaposing the histories of satellite transmission and remote sensing in India and Dubai, **Keller Easterling** unpacks the notion of the unified global village. Rather than a true internationalism, she reveals a complex picture of commercial and political alliances and networks that operate between national jurisdictions.

launch of an experimental satellite (1961) in response to *Sputnik 1* (1957). Sanctioned by the subsequent Satellite Communication Act of 1962, the Communication Satellite Corporation (COMSAT) launched *Early Bird*, the first of a six-satellite system, in 1965. Bouncing to the COMSAT system, new earth stations in the UK, France, Germany, Italy, Brazil and Japan broadcast the first global village transmission of the moon walk in 1969. INTELSAT, to which most countries now belong, collectively owns this infrastructure.[2] Yet there are also regional fleets orbiting the same equatorial Clarke Belt, named after their ambassador. Among these are RSCC, serving Russia and the CIS, EUTELSAT serving Europe, ARABSAT (1967) serving the Middle East and North Africa, INDOSAT (1967) serving Indonesia, and INSAT (1975) serving India.[3] Private consortiums such as SES Global, the largest satellite company in the world, own stakes in many regional and global companies.[4]

Futurologists imagined that satellites would allow developing countries to leapfrog into the developed world, bypassing investments in a conventional infrastructure grid by simply beaming down a communication infrastructure. Satellites would produce a digital pollen, or digital weather, of sorts, that would not be magnetised to any existing metropolitan formations. In the same way that dam building was thought to reorient infrastructures around a natural resource, satellites might be a resource stored in the air, returning benefits to all they touched regardless of previous urban and political structures. In *The Third Wave* (1980), in a chapter entitled 'Gandhi with Satellites', Alvin Toffler projected India's use of satellites as a possible exemplar. Correcting the mistakes of military industrial infrastructures, the fleet would insert high-performance technologies into very primitive rural environments to act as economic catalysers. With the elegiac and emotional

in 1972, not as competition for Russian or US space programmes with their space stations and manned exploration of extra-terrestrial planets. Instead, the targeted frontier was nation building.[6] Indeed, while the West let military agendas lead its initial satellite use, South Asia initially emphasised its use of satellite capabilities for earth sensing.

In 1975, the same year that HBO broadcast its first satellite downlink of an Ali/Frazier fight, an intercosmos rocket of the USSR launched the first Indian satellite, *Aryabhata*.[7] The political geography of the launches reflected India's stance of political nonalignment. In 1976, using an American satellite, *ATS-6*, India began an experimental programme called SITE (satellite

A satellite earth station in Hyderabad, India, demonstrates some of the peculiar architectural signals associated with broadcast urbanism.

The Cyber Gateway building is phase II of Hyderabad's HITEC city, a flagship venture in the projected transformation of Hyderabad to Cyberabad.

instructional television experiment) that broadcast TV for a year to 2,400 villages in the least developed areas.[8] From 1977 to 1979, India used Franco-German technology for another similar experiment called STEP.[9] The INSAT satellites, one of which was bought from ARABSAT, were launched in the 1980s with the help of the US and Europe. This system still broadcasts today.

While various pilot projects have delivered TV, data and government information, some of the most recent projects have focused on the software industry and remote sensing.[10] INSAT-1B allowed Doordarshan, the government television station, to set up a national network that focused not on regional or rural markets but, rather, on those in India's largest cities.[11] The government agency, Software Technology Parks of India (STPI), brokers bandwidth and enclave urbanism to a collection of global companies. Twenty-two earth stations generate IT gateways and bandwidth allotments in what constitutes a very special location. The time zone, when paired with that of the US, provides a 24-hour continuous work day. The location also yields wages that are approximately a quarter of those in the US.[12] Similarly, the National Remote Sensing Agency (NRSA) continues to map ground water, minerals, forests, ocean resources and land use in both urban and rural areas.[13] As it fed data about natural resources or weather directly back into an agricultural industry, remote sensing has truly fulfilled the agrarian dreams of futurologists. The NRSA has also been able to mobilise in the face of earthquakes and other natural disasters like the tsunami of 2004. Hyderabad, a burgeoning centre of software development, is also an important earth station for remote-sensing work as varied as building highways, predicting landslides and targeting ganja plantations.[14] Still, the technology has also been used to engineer controversial dam-building and water-management systems that may be tied to agriculture but are designed within World Bank boilerplates.

Remote sensing often piggybacks on the satellite needs of other industries such as IT. Global connectivity and the satellite urbanism of IT parks was one of the most successful masquerades used by the dangerous neotraditionalism of the Bharatiya Janata Party (BJP). Satellite networks continue to be an engine in India's competition with China over global presence. The same satellite instruments can be used not only for global IT alliances in Malaysia and the UAE, but in larger ecological neighbourhoods within which India may choose cooperation or autonomy. The India Space Research Organization (ISRO) has recently signed an agreement with a Malaysian company to jointly develop its

Remote-sensing image of Hugli River Delta, India.

Remote-sensing image of Calcutta.

own communications satellite and launch it from India. While designed for telecommunications, these satellites are also expected to deliver a remote-sensing 'payload' to a world that is hungry for various kinds of intelligence or environmental data. More importantly, India will take its place with the major players in global space initiatives: the US, UK, Russia, China, France, Germany and Japan.[15]

Nearby satellite neighbourhoods in the Middle East are launching their own satellites and have mixed remote sensing with some of the most unexpected and hyperbolic forms of nation building.[16] The late Sheik Zayed bin Sultan Al Nahyan is often remembered as a leader who was also a naturalist, falconer and preserver of the traditions of a coastal desert ecology. When Sheik Zayed of Abu Dhabi and Sheik Mohammed bin Rashid Al Maktoum of Dubai formed the Federation of the United Arab Emirates in 1971, they were intent on preserving regional traditions and diversifying the economy. The Emirates had just begun pumping oil in the 1960s. The possibilities for a public relations romance are obvious. As Arab music plays in the background and falcons fly overhead, a precious drop of water is engineered to create new oases of trees. As a million trees are planted, the UAE also becomes a leader in advancing desalination technologies and aluminium

production. A mirror-tiled, air-conditioned, modern urbanism is at once regional and global, willing to launder any identity and keep any secret. A country of nomadic and maritime habits is creating a place for a new and always temporary population of tourists.[17] Better than citizens or illegal workers, tourists can be screened and curated. Once inside, they do nothing but pass out their money – a year's worth of taxes in a relatively short period. The UAE is building every mirage of global tourism – theme parks, 'worlds' and entire island landmasses that make other extreme tourist parks in the world look like a didactic midway. Oil is never mentioned, except in the context of advancing remote-sensing technologies used to detect oil spills that might disturb coastal ecologies or desalination plants.

Remote-sensing satellites are ecological instruments that receive a central position in the government and in universities. The instrument upon which all of these developments rely is not only a vein of oil, but also a vein of microwaves. Many notable research organs and projects are dependent on this satellite constellation. One of these, the Environmental Research and Wildlife Development Agency (ERWDA), of which Sheik Zayed was deputy chairman, is designed to protect wildlife and natural ecologies in Abu Dhabi.[18] It is also being used to correct some global misconceptions about environmental abuse in developing countries. This is data that developing countries use to argue their environmental status in the world, since they are often ranked low in sustainability efforts.[19] Al Ain, a natural oasis and a pet project of Sheik Zayed, is the subject of a special remote-sensing project. As Zayed repopulated the forest of date palms here, remote-sensing satellites were used to track changes in the city as well as coastal areas from 1976 to 2000.[20] Efforts to combat desertification, and to preserve Sammaliah Island, a wildlife sanctuary near Abu Dhabi, are other notable experiments conducted by Al Ain's remote-sensing facility.[21] Farouk El Baz, director of remote sensing at Boston University, has been influential in the region, arguing for the use of technologies for regional ecological monitoring, and for finding opportunities to make these initiatives adjuncts to larger technology-park and free-trade-zone projects.[22]

More extreme are the uses of remote sensing and GIS in building compounds for global tourists and expatriates. Since 1999, the UAE has also begun building The Palms and The World, offshore island formations that are so large they will be visible from space. Promoted as the eighth wonder of the world, The Palms actually takes the form of date palms in silhouette. Each of the fronds emanates from a trunk of entertainment and resort buildings, and extends out into the water like a peninsular cul-de-sac, adding more than 120 kilometres of expensive coastline. Encircling the entire formation of fronds is an outer breakwater. An engineering feat, each of the shapes are made by compacted sand and rock dropped precisely from boats, while divers conduct the necessary underwater structural and environmental work. These instructions are delivered via GIS, and construction photos are delivered via remote sensing. Tourists and Western expats populate the ads in print and online.[23]

The World, using a similar engineering technique, creates an archipelago that takes the shape of the world's continents. On these islands, owners from anywhere in the world may create anything from a private compound to a resort. Some islands will mimic the glamorous global locations to which they correspond geographically. The World also advertises complete privacy and safety for its offshore owners and tenants by providing a small fleet of security boats charged to continuously troll the waters between islands.

Remote sensing provides an extraterrestrial set of tools and eyes for constructing collaborations that are truly global in scale and embedded in networks that operate between national jurisdictions. Yet the result is not a global village of cooperation, but a segregated and politicised set of microwave neighbourhoods. They may all be broadcasting Zee TV and Star TV into resort hotels in South Asia, Southeast Asia and the Middle East, but they are jurisdictionally incapable of delivering a tsunami warning with several hours of lead time. Still, if there ever was an instrument simultaneously tied to protective national military technologies and an equally protective need for global ecological cooperation, it would be satellite technologies. Pliant in the face of many masquerades, this technology may be an unwitting party to some partial desegregation of global networks. Δ

Coastline of Dubai showing the offshore island for the Burj Al Arab, the photogenic tall building that regularly appears in Dubai's global postcard portraits.

Notes
1 www.lyngsat.com/headlines.shtml.
2 www.hq.nasa.gov/office/pao/History/satcomhistory.html.
3 www.indosat.com/iframes_page.asp?konten=About_Corp_Brief.htm&kanan=about; and M Richharia, *Satellite Communications Systems: Design Principles*, McGraw-Hill (New York), 1999, p 3. ASIASAT (1988) was Asia's first privately owned regional fleet. www.asiasat.com.
4 www.ses-global.com/corporate/index.htm.
5 Alvin Toffler, 'Gandhi with Satellites', *The Third Wave*, William Morrow and Company, Inc (New York), 1980, p 362. Toffler writes, quoting Jagdish Kapur writing in *India 2000 AD*: 'A new balance has now to be struck between "the most advanced science and technology available to the human race" and "the Gandhian vision of the idyllic green pastures, the village republics". Such a practical combination, Kapur declares, requires a "total transformation of the society, its symbols and values, its system of education, its incentives, the flow of its energy resources, its scientific and industrial research and a whole lot of other institutions".'
6 www.isro.org/about_isro.htm.
7 www.geo-orbit.org/sizepgs/geodef.html#anchor1302357
8 David Page and Willian Crawley, *Satellites over South Asia: Broadcasting Culture and the Public Interest*, Sage Publications (New Delhi), 2001, p 65.
9 www.isro.org/old_sat.htm#site.
10 www.isro.org/sat.htm#insat.
11 Ibid. INSAT-1A in 1982 and INSAT-1B in 1983. INSAT-1A lasted for only six months, and subsequent satellites, INSAT-1C launched by the European Ariane vehicle, lasted only one and a half years. The INSAT-1D, launched by the US, is still in service. INSAT now also has INSAT 2A-E and INSAT-3A-E.
12 John Stremlau, 'Dateline Bangalore: Third World Technopolis', *Foreign Policy* 102, Spring 1996, pp 152–69. Srinagar, Moahli Shimia, Delhi, Noida, Jaipu, Indore, Ganhinagar, Calcutta, Bhubaneswar, Navi Mumbai, Aurangabad, Pune, Hyderabad, Bisag, Manipal Bangalore, Chennai, Coimbatore, Mysore and Thiruvananthapuram are among the earth stations.
13 www.nrsa.gov.in/engnrsa/aboutus/organization.html.
14 Indo-Asian News Service, 5 January 2005; *Hindustan Times*, 5 January 2005.
15 *Business Today*, 13 March 2005, p 132.
16 Xinhua General News Service, 29 June 2004; Emirates News Agency, 7 December 2004.
17 www.sheikh-zayed.info/3275; www.uae.gov.ae/Government/sheik_zayed.htm.
18 *The Emirates*, 21 February 2001.
19 Ibid, 3 July 2002.
20 Ibid, 24 July 2004; *Gulf News*, 9 June 2004.
21 *Gulf News*, 22 June 2003; Emirates News Agency, 29 December 2004.
22 *Gulf News*, 22 May 2002; www.dailystar.com.lb/article.asp?edition_id=10&categ_id=5&article_id=14061.
23 www.palmisland.co.ae/swf/main.html.

Shrines and Satellites: Doshi's Aranya District, Indore

The word 'aranya', which means 'forest' in Hindi, is an apt name for the incremental mixed-income housing project in Indore designed by Balkrishna Doshi. It reveals the architect's intention that the project should grow slowly, from the bottom up – a social, as well as an economic and architectural goal. As Doshi argues: 'The indigenous character of built form provides a setting for the continuation of the fundamental values of society'.[1] Twenty years after its inception, Aranya provides an ideal site for studying the effects of recent societal changes in India, as reflected in domestic architecture, specifically because the tightness of its spaces forces an extreme condensation and layering of the local and the remote.

In the areas of Aranya designed for the lowest income group, small courtyards intended for community use break up long rows of tiny 12- x 32-foot residential plots. In these courtyards, as well as in many of the homes, temples and shrines have been built where daily prayers connect residents to the cosmos and to their immutable, caste-determined place within society. These sites of ancient ritual frequently share spaces with devices that bring the cosmos back to the residents: satellite TV, mobile phones and computers with Internet connections.

Ironically, the physical infrastructure at Aranya is functioning poorly: residents must collect water daily from taps in the street, storm drains frequently back up, and wild pigs are a main form of garbage disposal. Yet the healthy communications infrastructure (both worldly and divine) that has developed in these difficult conditions demonstrates the power of bottom-up development to reveal rapidly changing societal values.

Note
1 Vastu-Shilpa Foundation for Studies and Research in Environmental Design, *Aranya: An Approach to Settlement Design*, Housing & Urban Development Corporation and the Vastu-Shilpa Foundation (Ahmedabad), 1990, p 15.

This loft-style house, designed by its owner, is unusual in that it makes use of an open plan to accommodate multiple uses in a small space. The kitchen is upstairs, while the main downstairs space functions as living room, sleeping room and office.

Most residents park their motorcycles and scooters inside their houses at night to protect them, allowing the living room/bedroom to double as a garage for part of the day.

Cows, sacred animals to Hindus, are well looked after by the local community. They have become so accustomed to this arrangement that they often pop in to remind residents that it's dinner time.

One of the many small temples that have popped up in the open spaces reserved for community use in Aranya. Such a temple serves not only as a place of prayer, but also provides a visual and social focal point for residents.

Even the simplest of interiors will usually contain a television and a stereo.

In low-income areas, water is available from a tap in the street for about an hour a day. As most residents are outside collecting water at this time, local vendors take advantage of the opportunity to sell their goods.

Residents often build shrines in their homes that may be dedicated to a particular god or contain images of ancestors. The shrines share the space of the room with beds, televisions, sewing machines, computers, and motorcycles parked inside for safe keeping.

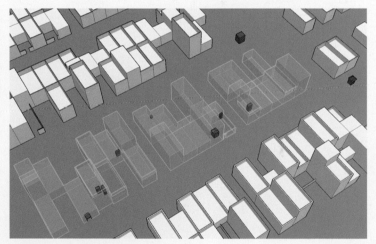

A low-income block showing the distribution of shrines in houses and temples in outdoor common areas.

In a local gym, a poster of the owner, an Indian champion weightlifter, shares equal billing with Hanuman, the Hindu god of power and strength.

COCHIN, INDIA

May Joseph draws a poetic portrait of Cochin, in southern India, a contemporary city overlaid with history and successive migrations. Old and new collide with the local and regional pulls of cultures and peoples, the diaspora being further heightened by the possibilities of telecommunications matrixes and media transmission.

NOTES FROM A NERVE OF THE WORLD

Hemmed in by stone walls precise and systematic, made impressive by reclamations of slough and slew, Cochin, a city of islands, recedes and rises, like its waterline, on the Kerala coast of south India. The city undulates, ensconced between hulls of sisal and coir, etched with stone markings of former visitations – Chinese, Arab, African, Persian, the sounds of Portuguese, the signs of Hebrew. Displaced fantasies of Le Corbusier and Richard Meier now interrupt the transitioning skyline of low-lying structures as glass and steel, concrete and plastic assert the arrogant prominence of a vertical imaginary, simulations of another Asian megacity framed by Dutch urban planning – a Manhattan in Malabar.

City of Dispersals

Koji, kochi, cochim, cochin: the city morphs memories, boundaries and genealogies as gods seek refuge from empires, holy men embrace nirvana, pirates plunder for black gold and modern nomads embrace modernity's democratic promises. This axis of medieval and Enlightenment encounters claims a standing still, a quiet place from which to ferment a future without blood, mortar, guns and ships, absent slaves and their curses. The ruins of older collisions hold to ransom the storm beneath the calm: a solitary synagogue, a decaying Buddha, tormented St Sebastian derelict and forgotten, posters of Lenin and Stalin, hammer and sickle graffiti, rumours of hurried leavings and surreptitious beginnings.

A central node of the maritime world of a bygone era, Cochin is a city perpetually in transition. Its history is multiple, journeys to a somewhere – inscriptions in a torah; a 14th-century Portuguese statue of St Sebastian, a Zanzibari cap, an Omani minaret, a Wendy's pizza parlour, cybercafés and high-tech malls in cerulean blue and fuchsia. Now land-bound, now ocean-bound, now email-bound, now cell-phone-bound, it is a city of stormy contradictions. From Macao and Mombasa, Belem and Muscat they came with dreams and dervishes – Ibn Battuta and Vasco da Gama, Captain Kidd and Marco Polo – to invent a traveller's city where Muslims, Christians, Hindus and Jews, Buddhists, Jains, Trotskyites and anarchists jostle a modernity held fast in the fulcrum of maritime economies. Silk, cardamom, cloves and the treacherous pepper bewitch time and intoxicate history.

These days, a glittery spartanism grips Cochin in thrall as gold, diamonds, chiffon and technology evoke a fetish for the new. Consumption and the culture of obsolescence is seducing this Marxist city towards its uneasy identity as a transnational hub, with its speculative architecture, delectable bakeries, confectioners, designer shoe shops, art galleries, thriving tourist economy, tropical climate, alternative health remedies, Ayurvedic massage centres and rich cultural traditions of dance, theatre, music and martial arts.

Ecumenical City

One enters the city as a fragment. Marxist. Mercantilist. Trader, tourist or traveller. Circling the city through cumulonimbus clouds, the eye catches glimpses of landscape: waterways, canals, islands, lakes, rivers, water pools, slivers of isthmuses, an archipelago of lush swampland. Cochin is a mnemonic reminder of Manhattan before its verticality: Jew Street, Muslim Street, Broadway, Spice Street, Broad Street, Linden Street and Parsley Street. Its 16th-century claim to fame is its impressive natural harbour, one of the largest in the Asian maritime economy and worthy of Henry Hudson's awe.

The Malabar coast is notoriously turbulent with no calm havens for precolonial and colonial travellers coming from Macao, the South China Seas, Batavia and Malacca through the Coromandel coast around Cape Comorin. However, Cochin emerges in early depictions as a haven of peace, a monsoon city of pagodas, minarets, domes and cupolas, spires, towers and Modernist hopes, whose mouldy roofs erode the dank of dark tales· fervent conversions, rapes of the pagan, concubinage without consequence. Embossed upon the city is the mystique of the Franciscans, the intensity of the Jesuits, the severity of the Syrians, and the decadence of the Romans (who landed in Cranganore, referred to by Ptolemy and Pliny as Museri). Invoking Lusitania and Malabar, the Arabian Sea and the Indian Ocean, Soviet communism and Cuban socialism, Moscow and Mecca, mobile phones and outsourcing, Cochin is a mendicant city – a nerve of the world.

Port City

To live in Manhattan is to live through the memories of other port cities one has inhabited: Dar es Salaam, Cochin, Recife. These cities have been influenced to varying degrees by Dutch urban planning, Portuguese architecture, indigenous reclamations. To write about Cochin is to write through the histories of Batavia, Macao, Hoi An, Aceh, Malacca, Colombo, Mombasa, Aleppo, Manhattan.

Cochin is a series of urban centres linked through commerce, like Los Angeles. It is a conglomeration of islands, waterways, town and village systems of urban intensities linked through history and geology, like New York City. Its physical geography invokes the structure of Amsterdam's Harbour Islands. The Dutch built the Eastern Islands around the city of Amsterdam to expand their colonial port city infrastructure: Kattenburg, Wittenburg and Oostenburg (and recently, KNSM Eiland, Java Eiland, Borneo Eiland,

Fort Cochin, India
Yellow-reddish in hue, the buildings of Fort Cochin are mnemonic reminders of the Dutch and Portuguese encounters. Built primarily by the Dutch at the same time as New Amsterdam in the 1640s, these high-walled, narrow-windowed homes formerly nestled within a walled community now the location of commercial exporters of tea and spices.

Sporenburg). They mirror their creations in Cochin through their fascination with Vypin Island (Fort New Orange), Fort Cochin, Bolghatty Island and Vallarpadam. The Portuguese built fort cities of strategic significance, reproducing their penchant for geological liminalities of the Algarve: isthmus, jutting rocks, spectacular vistas of maritime reconnaissance grounded by churches of the Order of Santiago. The British usurp Cochin with gunpowder and treachery to establish a mirror port to their other colonial outpost, New York. They build a simulation of Manhattan within Cochin and call it Willingdon Island.

Cochin is unique and a replica, it is an Indian Ocean city awake across multiple temporal structures from the 16th and 21st centuries, the maritime and aerospace economies of time and space. It is a microcosm of the first throes of globalisation spanning the 9th-century Buddhist migrations to Borobodhur, Angkor Wat and Ayuthaya, the 13th-century trading economies of the Omanis, Africans and the Chinese, the pre-Inquisition migration of the Black Jews and the 16th-century colonial conquests by the West.

Densities/Distensions
Today, Cochin is many cities in one. Water defines its logic as the city finds itself at the liminal crossroads of three oceans: the Indian Ocean, the Arabian Sea and the Bay of Bengal. Cochin is consequently a commercial and a historic city, structured around a man-made archipelago on the tempestuous Malabar coast. Nodes of intensity structure its bridges, railway junctions, ferry jetties, port, trading villages and settler outposts of formerly Portuguese, Jewish, Dutch, British, Arab, Chinese, Yemeni, Syrian, African and, more recently, Tamil, Gujarati, and Sindhi communities now incorporated into the larger Cochin mosaic. Departures, relocations and commutes mark daily life in Cochin, reiterating its

nomadic structuring as a city of nonlinear and fractured segments, rather than a conventional urban core.

Cochin is a composite of Abu Dhabi, Dubai, Bahrain, Kuala Lumpur, Bangkok, Hong Kong, Dar-es-salaam, Muscat, Aden, Basra, Kuwait and New York, as migrants leave families behind in the city in states of deferral. It is a euphemism for the quintessential contemporary condition of spatial dislocation emblematised by the Dar-es-salaam Mosque in Ernakulam, Cochin's sister city. The twin cities of Cochin and Ernakulam fragment the city's sense of itself into historic and contemporary enclaves, a cartography that is elliptical and perambulatory rather than grid-like. Cochin is a district, as well as a city, with two urban cores – Cochin and Ernakulam. The areas of Mattanchery and Fort Cochin, embody the medieval and colonial city, while Thopumpody functions as a distended mobile link between the old city of Fort Cochin, Willingdon Island and the strung-out commercial port city of Ernakulam, whose own historicity has merged into the greater metropolitan area of the city of Cochin.

The idea of Cochin is awash in movement. Its construction is one of simultaneous habitation, multisited between maritime-, air- and land-bound circuits. Life in the city involves movement between islands, traversals across old and new landscapes, between the past and the present, hard to see and deeply interwoven. Lifestyles incorporate multiple modes of transport. A university lecturer's daily routine entails taking a boat from Bolghatty Island across to the main ferry terminal in Ernakulam, and from there a bus to the train station in Ernakulam, then a train from Ernakulam to Allepey where she teaches, in the evening returning home by train, bus and boat. A doctor from Vypin

Market Street, Cochin, India
Colourful plastic calling cards, inflatable Spiderman dolls, *The Last Supper*, sound systems and vivacious brooms are among the bric-a-brac that accosts the eye when passing by the cluster of Chinese stores on Market Street, remnants of what was once a thriving Chinese immigrant community in Cochin. Its most influential legacy is the Chinese fishing nets that dot the coastline along Vembanad Lake and out into the Lakshadeep Sea.

Island takes the ferry to Ernakulam, then a bus to work. A massage therapist commutes between Allepey, an hour south of Cochin, and the city, by taking a boat and two buses, returning via the same route at weekends.

Many in the city have a parent, child or member of their extended family in either Southeast Asia, the Middle East or Africa. In this state of deferral, all sensations are refracted by distance, where the loss of a loved one is mediated by the telephone, the hurried expensive flight back for a delayed burial and a hasty return to the grind of living without time for grieving. Daily life for many Cochinis is a state of longing and nostalgia, as families live in the present awaiting the sporadic, infrequent and intermittent return of their loved ones. This is a narrative as old as the city itself.

To live in Cochin is to live in an interrelated structure of urban linkages of local densities, regional intensities across the Malabar coast, particularly from Cochin to Kollam (Quilon – a major port city during the 13th century, now a quiet seaside town) and international labour flows. Old colonial spice routes collide with modern migrational itineraries to East Asia, Africa and the Middle East. Doctors, lawyers, accountants, dentists, labourers, drivers, nurses, teachers and engineers represent a critical mass of the flexible migrant population, generating new relationships of habitation and immigration that are only tenuously located in the language of diaspora. These nomadic populations of individuals with familial links to Kerala and tenuous lives in other continents are symptomatic of the deeply fracturing relationships to space and memory, family and movement emerging in postcolonial cities. Some migrants dwell in little enclaves of masculinity or, more precariously, as women domestics, nurses and teachers in Dubai, Muscat, Bangkok and Dar-es-salaam, while also inhabiting emotive lives in Kerala or in yet a third country, such as the US or UK, cemented through the sojourns of a husband, son or sister. These fraught experiences of migrant Cochinis abroad throw open the vulnerable sphere of contemporary Cochin, at once locatable within the boundaries of the definable city, and displaced onto other locales in countries such as Iraq, Afghanistan, Hong Kong and Sierra Leone, where Cochinis live and work.

Contemporary Cochin is an expression of its transport-networked practices of how people live the everyday: boat systems, railway networks, telecommunications matrixes, bus routes, familial inter-city connections, televised phantasmatics and mnemonic routes. It is a liminal end-nerve in the contemporary global economy, and a centripetal catalyst from an earlier globalisation of the 13th century. It lives in the here and now of Gulf money, African sojourns, Malaysian tourist jaunts, Kuwaiti commercialism, Muscat banking, American dreams and the trace of the historic past. ⏃

> To live in Cochin is to live in an interrelated structure of urban linkages of local densities, regional intensities across the Malabar coast, and international labour flows.

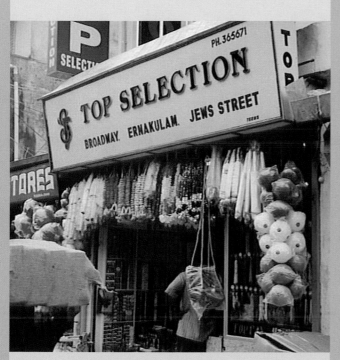

Jew Street, Ernakulam, India
A major commercial artery of Ernakulam, Jew Street echoes an older Jew Street in Fort Cochin located in the Jewish quarter of the city where there exists one of the oldest Jewish synagogues in Asia. Jew Street in Ernakulam is a vivid street filled with clothing, textile, industrial, car and fashion commodities.

Spice Street, Cochin, India
Fragrant aromas of cardamom, cloves and ginger waft through crowded Spice Street, where pepper, nutmeg and cinnamon, among other spices, compete for their place in the world export market. The geographical and colonial associations evoked by these spices encapsulate the Indian Ocean from Zanzibar, where cloves are manufactured, and Colombo, the primary port where cinnamon is harvested, to Kollam where pepper is grown, and Jakarta where nutmeg is cultivated.

Circling Around the Multi-National City: Silicon Valley, New York and New Delhi

Silicon Valley in northern California, New York's internal suburbias, and Gurgaon, a burgeoning corporate city outside New Delhi, are all caught within the feedback loops of globalisation. They are stops in transit through the 'multi-national city' (MNC – also an acronym for multi-national corporation). The MNC is a city indifferent to national borders, made up of office buildings, call centres, gated residential enclaves, shopping malls, electronic screens, and other such artefacts spread across the world.

First stop is sunny Silicon Valley, whose financial climate has rocked from boom to bust to everything in between. Brand names stretch the length of the highway: Oracle, Adobe, Cisco, SGI, Apple, and so on, with industrial units occupied to varying degrees depending on the economic climate. Vast parking lots and outdoor spaces are unavoidable. They are generally empty and seemingly calm, irrespective of the (economic or geological) climate.

However, far from calm is the euphoria encountered at the second stop along this route: New York. Famous for its tough street life, New York is also the site of slow transformations to a suburbia previously unimagined, evidenced by its shiny new shopping malls and megastores, and by its new reputation as one of the most tourist-friendly cities in the world.

Such suburbias are also reflected far away in the new malls outside of New Delhi, our third stop. The offices of DLF City/Gurgaon – developed by a private company, the Delhi Land Finance Group – are back offices for multi-nationals from around the world: American Express, GE, Dell, Citibank and Nestlé to name just a few. Office towers and gated high-rise apartment blocks float across a semirural landscape. Unlike Silicon Valley, where basic infrastructure came before corporate sprawl, DLF City is developing in reverse. A major highway is still in construction, and many tall buildings are still serviced by dirt roads and remain dependent on private back-up electrical generators.

And so we travel between cultures and time zones, following the loops that hold these cities together as well as keep them apart. Our circles around the MNC thus circle around the question: Where are we going? And also ask: What is to be done?

Excerpts from Reinhold Martin and Kadambari Baxi, *Multi-National City: Architectural Itineraries*, forthcoming. This is a guidebook to the future of architecture and of the city, by way of three itineraries through three cities and their histories. Each tour ends with a brief, an unannounced stop at a project (Feedback) designed by Martin/Baxi Architects, which applies the lessons of the MNC to itself.

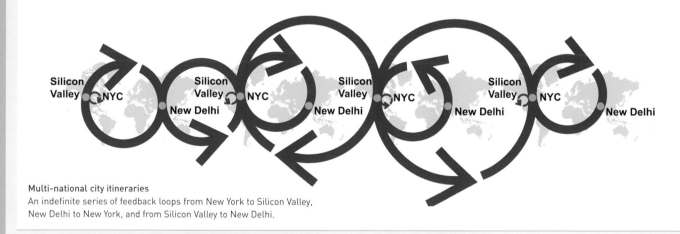

Multi-national city itineraries
An indefinite series of feedback loops from New York to Silicon Valley, New Delhi to New York, and from Silicon Valley to New Delhi.

Multi-national city 'monuments' in Silicon Valley, New York City and DLF City (Gurgaon/New Delhi)
Corporate headquarters, offices, call centres, apartment towers and logos.

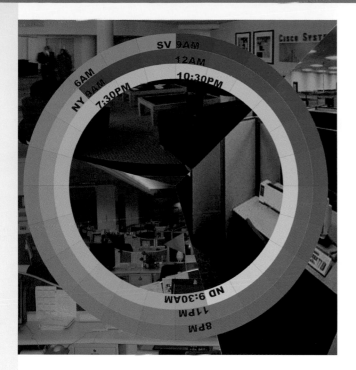

Multi-national city time zones and interiors: call centre/office workers in Silicon Valley, New York City and DLF City (Gurgaon/New Delhi) linked by a 24-hour work cycle

1 A typical day in the life of an office worker (Silicon Valley)
'As Phillips worked she didn't need to worry about running errands to the drugstore or the car wash. All material needs were satisfied inside the lettered monoliths [the Cisco buildings]. If she needed breakfast, she could go to the company cafeteria as early as 7am ... All and sundry goods could be purchased at McWhorters Express Store in Building J ... At the edge of the cubes on Phillips' floor, and in the other alphabetized edifices, stood the break room. Each break room housed one of the fabled refrigerators of many sodas, the free panoply of nonalcoholic beverages. If Phillips needed some pants pressed, she would go to the break room ... A jaunt from Building A to Building L would provide quite a workout, but not as good as the one she could get at the gym housed in Building L ... Her car was pampered, too, with onsite washes and oil changes. Cisco provided her with all these perks so that she could spend as much time doing her job as possible.'[1]
(From David Bunnell, *Making the Cisco Connection*, John Wiley & Sons (New York), 2000, pp 92–3)

2 A typical night in the life of a call-centre worker (DLF City, Gurgaon/New Delhi)
'Meghna is a 23-year-old call center operator somewhere in Gurgaon. When her phone rings, she becomes "Michelle". The caller is in Philadelphia, asking for a credit extension: Meghna is unruffled. Months of training, which included watching Hollywood blockbusters to pick up a wide variety of American accents and reading John Grisham thrillers to clear any linguistic obstacles, have paid off. Her computer screen even flashes the weather at Philadelphia as she tells a caller what a perfect day it is. Meghna signs off saying, "Have a good day". Outside her window it is pitch dark.'
(From Raj Chengappa and Milini Goyal, 'Housekeepers of the World', *India Today*, New Delhi, 2002, p 10.)

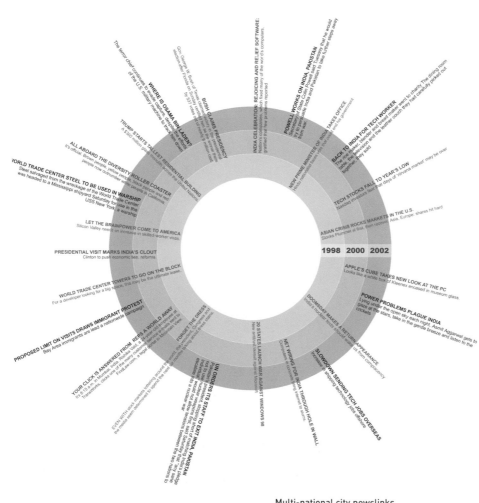

Multi-national city newslinks
Selected news headlines from online news archives.

Top/bottom scenarios
'World-class' building tops with distinct bottom realities: the Adobe headquarters in Silicon Valley, Citibank in New York City, and the DLF Tower in Gurgaon/New Delhi.

Speculations
What is to be done? Future ghosted. Formerly Oracle. Formerly 3COM. Formerly Intel. (From the Feedback projects by Martin/Baxi Architects, 2001–04).

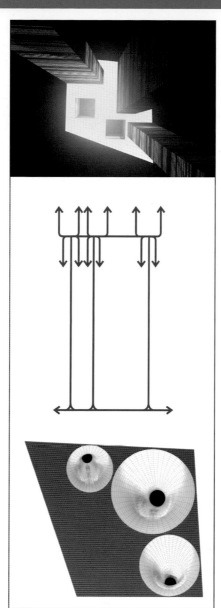

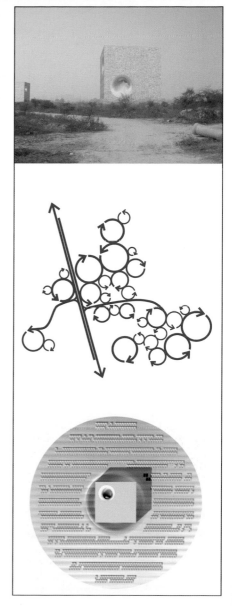

Martin/Baxi Architects, Feedback, 2001–04
Feedback CVRP (Silicon Valley), Feedback WTC (New York), Feedback DLF (Gurgaon/New Delhi).
The Feedback projects apply the lessons of MNC to itself. A site circulation system in circles
is proposed in Silicon Valley. A 9/11 memorial may be seen from below in a tower with an
upside-down access tree in New York. In New Delhi, cube buildings sit on circular zones
with a typical zero-sum game: parking vs solar panels. The interiors of these offices are
punctuated with MNC accessories: potted plants, empty couches and palm trees.

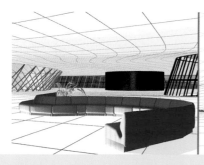

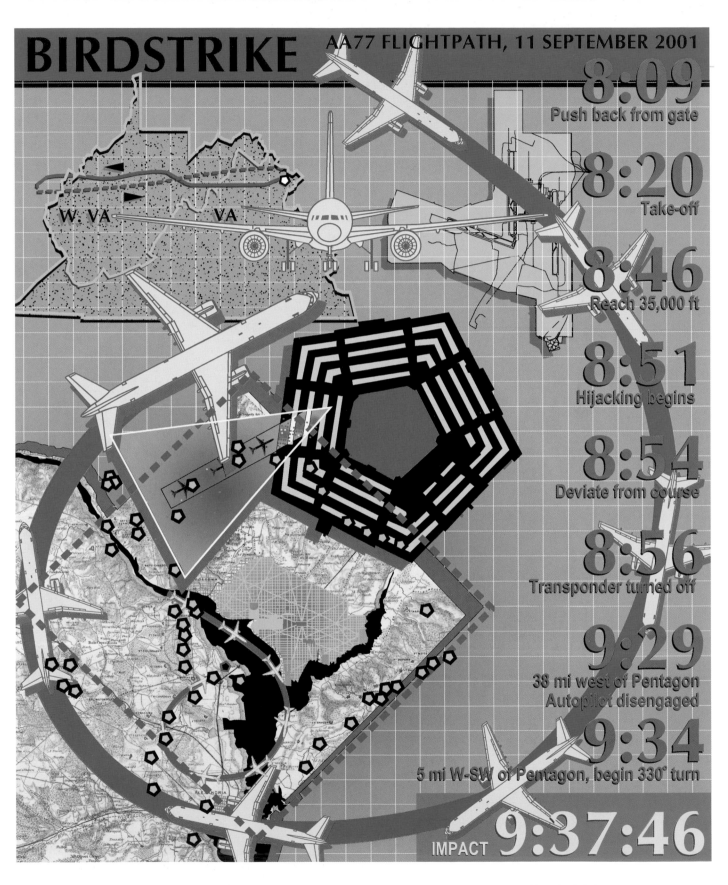

BIRDSTRIKE

AA77 FLIGHTPATH, 11 SEPTEMBER 2001

8:09 Push back from gate

8:20 Take-off

8:46 Reach 35,000 ft

8:51 Hijacking begins

8:54 Deviate from course

8:56 Transponder turned off

9:29 38 mi west of Pentagon Autopilot disengaged

9:34 5 mi W-SW of Pentagon, begin 330° turn

IMPACT **9:37:46**

W. VA   VA

The 11 September flight path of hijacked AA77 linked two major anchors of Northern Virginia sprawl: Dulles International Airport (1962) and the Pentagon (1943), gateway to the area's prominent defence presence. The airliner's final overflight of urbanised landscapes culminated in an earthbound spiral that retraced the circumferential geometry of the Civil War fort system known as the Defenses of Washington.

NATIONAL SECURITY SPRAWL
WASHINGTON DC

Battlements and fortifications are most often associated with the historic cities of the Old World. Here, **Deborah Natsios** gives an account of the physical and virtual transformations that have affected Greater Washington DC since 9/11.

Birdstrike

Greater Washington DC's airspace offers strategic overviews of tangled metropolitan landscapes shaped by the exigencies of successive national security paradigms. In the hour before it crashed into the west facade of the Pentagon at 9:38 am on 11 September 2001, hijacked American Airlines flight 77 mapped a provocative trajectory above this complex domain, tracking national security landmarks embedded in one of the nation's fastest-growing urbanised formations.[1] Within the hour, the capital region's snarled American-dream sprawl would be transformed into the unprecedented threatscape of the 'homeland'.

The Los Angeles-bound flight had headed west from suburban Dulles International Airport before stealthily doubling back towards the capital city with its transponder deactivated,[2] navigating a final overflight of Northern Virginia's anarchic exurban terrain. Beneath the opportunistic flight path, national security institutions and defence contractors lay discreetly camouflaged within a congested topography of subdivisions, big-box retailers, cineplexes, regional malls and information technology hubs.

At Dulles' southern perimeter, in Chantilly, Virginia, the National Reconnaissance Office (NRO) – maker of the country's classified spy satellites – huddled in a once clandestine $350-million suburban headquarters.[3] The NRO shared a paradigmatic suburban enclave with its top contractors, including Aerospace Corporation, Northrop Grumman and Lockheed Martin – the pastoral embellishments of an 'exclusive master-planned business community with state-of-the-art business setting amidst an environment with expansive green spaces, parks, ponds and trails'.[4] Closer to the Pentagon, in Langley, the Central Intelligence Agency (CIA) – developer of *CORONA*,[5] the nation's first photoreconnaissance satellite system – was sequestered in a complex modelled on an academic campus prototype.

Surrounded by evocatively seigneurial neighbourhoods – Savile Manor, Downcrest and Rokeby Farm – the CIA had taken refuge in suburban standards that codified the spatial and functional isolation of properties. Freestanding structures set back on greenscaped plots invited convenient anonymity rather than interaction.

Guided by a bird's-eye view of autumnal landscapes and the glinting Potomac River wending below, hijackers manoeuvred the Boeing 767 towards the pentagonal fortress at the margins of the capital's exemplary geometries. In the last minutes of the flight, a catastrophic earthbound spiral from an altitude of 7,000 feet collapsed institutional distinctions that stubbornly segregated aerial from terrestrial intelligence collection – as reconnaissance's privileged eye-in-the-sky was crushed into the earthbound object of its predatory scrutiny.

Long before Flight 77 tracked Northern Virginia's defence topography, the region was first surveyed by air in 1861 when a Union balloon hovering near Arlington helped orchestrate a successful attack against Confederate troops.[6] In intervening years, aerial and satellite technologies imaged the region's unruly growth for civilian applications, informing contentious processes of regional planning, traffic analysis and environmental evaluation. After 11 September, Greater Washington would submit to a new generation of 'persistent surveillance', including the military's experimental use of sensor-equipped blimps for aerial command-and-control.[7]

War Sprawl

The Department of Defense bulwark targeted on 11 September had provided the principal gateway for Northern Virginia's defence development on its completion in 1943, attracting dense clusters of contractors to its perimeter in Arlington County. These included the hijacked aircraft's own manufacturer, the Boeing Corporation, which, with contracts totalling $13.3 billion, was the nation's second-ranked vendor in 2001.[8]

Expansion of Greater Washington's government bureaucracies and technocracies, of regional infrastructures, settlements and

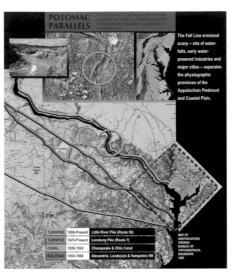

Defence contractors cluster along the District of Columbia's corridors of power, around the Pentagon in Arlington and, most recently, in edge-city nodes that coincide with Fairfax County's Special Planning Districts. Post 11 September, security regulations will alter this pattern as Department of Defense personnel in leased spaces relocate to secure sites further from the capital. Defence contractors are expected to follow, a migration that would exacerbate the regional effects of sprawl.

The Potomac River's 75-foot drop at Great Falls – situated along the East Coast's Fall Line erosional scarp – impeded efficient navigation, contributing to the development of parallel transport technologies and infrastructures that supported subsequent exurbanisation. These included turnpike, canal and railroad.

A 1930s proposal to recycle Civil War-era military roads and forts into a circumferential roadway would have adapted military artefacts to address expanding civilian needs. The circular scheme is reprised in the 64-mile-long I-495, the Capital Beltway (1961–4). Its origins as a National Defence Highway designed to move military equipment and personnel, and allow mass evacuation of the city in the event of nuclear attack, required that its diameter exceed a thermonuclear detonation centred on the capital.

population, had accelerated with security crises[9] from the Civil War through the two world wars, the Korean conflict, Cold War, Vietnam and current Middle East campaigns. Defence installations and symbiotic contractors would become a mainstay of the area's economy. By 2004, TRW, Raytheon, Lockheed Martin, Northrop Grumman and DynCorp alone employed more than 100,000 workers around the region.[10] Spurred by government-related employment – much of it linked to the national security sector – Greater Washington had by 2001 evolved into a mostly suburban metropolitan formation of 6,000 square miles with a population approaching 6,000,000.[11]

At the height of the Cold War, defence development invaded Fairfax County with the completion of Dulles International Airport (1962), the National Defense Highway System's circumferential Capital Beltway (1964) – its diameter calculated to exceed a thermonuclear detonation centred on the capital – and new CIA headquarters (1962). Anticipating unprecedented scales of consumerism, another 1960s landmark emerged minutes from the CIA. At the nexus of the emerging car culture – the confluence of the Beltway and three major highways – the country's first regional megamall was established at Tysons Corner. Within a generation, a new urbanised typology would accrete around the mall's core. The edge city – a building pattern defined as having at least 5 million square feet of leasable office space and at least 600,000 square feet of leasable retail space – introduced a significant suburban phenomenon: more jobs than bedrooms.[12]

Today, Tysons Corner's edge-city jobs include leading defence employers Raytheon, BAE Systems, DynCorp, Bechtel, Northrop Grumman and Science Applications International, who share real estate with the 'largest mass of retail operations on the East Coast, after Manhattan's'.[13] Purchasers of stand-off weapons,

early-warning systems and hostile-artillery location systems can also shop at Banana Republic, Brooks Brothers and the Disney Store.[14] The convergence of national security, transportation and consumer infrastructures was the defining armature of Northern Virginia's suburban expansion.

Miles from the capital's triumphalist monuments and circumspect war memorials, artefacts of the national security infrastructure have been normalised within suburban landscapes. Civil War forts were absorbed into the capital's arcadian park system. The W-83 Nike missile launch facility became a neighbourhood landmark in Great Falls, Virginia. A microwave station of the US Army Strategic Communications Command towers over the malls at Tysons Corner.[15]

If the District of Columbia was the emblematic centre of defence policy, the suburbs hosted the evolving war industry – a war machine made banal by the very real-estate market forces that were shaping the anonymous complexities of sprawl.

Home Invasion

The 11 September attack inaugurated a new chapter in a regional history that had seen metropolitan growth surge with evolving security paradigms. The landmarks of Pierre-Charles L'Enfant's seminal plan of 1791 – tangible symbols of democracy, national unity and power – were deemed vulnerable. The National Capital Planning Commission, overseer of urban design and preservation, introduced to the monumental core an aestheticised arsenal – hardened street furniture, bollards and plinth walls – to fortify building perimeters.[16] Jersey barriers and reinforced

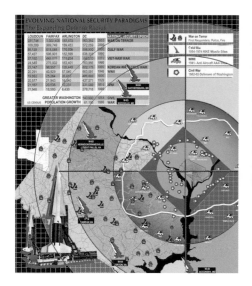

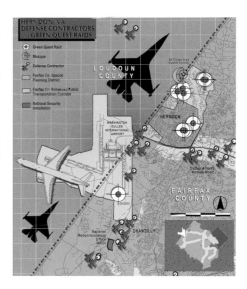

The defence systems of the 19th and early 20th century circumscribed the capital city, framing its centralised form. Sprawl's diffuse urbanisation introduces a new paradigm for the 21st-century homeland's defence: the national security apparatus is superimposed onto geographically dispersed civilian infrastructures, including police and fire services newly designated as paramilitary 'first responders'.

Since the 19th century, the Potomac River has offered a strategic link to Chesapeake Bay and the Atlantic coast. Waterfront defence posts have endured beyond the river's active military role, with the riparian edge providing a secure buffer for sensitive sites.

The 19th-century dairy-farming village of Herndon, Virginia, began its transformation into one of the capital's outer boom suburbs with the arrival, in 1859, of the railroad link to Alexandria. The self-described 'information technology hub with small-town charm' became the focus of government attention when homes and workplaces clustered near Dulles Airport were targeted by Operation Green Quest raids on 20 March 2002.

planters frame the new blastproof streetscape. Street and sidewalk closures limited public access to sensitive locations. Roadblocks and checkpoints challenged motorists and pedestrians. 'Flexibility and choice' are diminished in a city whose foundational master plan promoted transparency, vision and access.[17]

With the goal of safeguarding high-value targets of the capital's symbolic core, aggressive protocols were also deployed to manage the chaotic landscapes of the metropolitan periphery. The anarchic civilian geography of outlying suburbs would be subjected to provocative security interventions as sprawl's diffuse spaces were disciplined by the capital city's emerging technologies of political control. Invasive technologies threatened to perforate citizenship's privileged constitutional envelope,[18] however, jeopardising legal protections surrounding the coveted emblem of individual rights: the single-family home on its consecrated plot of primal green.

Transgressive enforcement methodologies were exhibited on a cloudy morning in March 2002, when 150 heavily armed federal agents invaded Northern Virginia's fragmented sprawl. Fanning out across scattered settlements west of Washington DC and watershed landscapes south of the Potomac, they conducted raids on a dozen area residences, businesses and nonprofit organisations.[19] Targeted sites included single-family homes and office buildings in Fairfax County, most clustered together conspicuously near Dulles Airport in the 'boom town' of Herndon, on the Loudoun County border.

Acting on an alleged 'criminal conspiracy to provide material support to terrorist organisations by a group of Middle Eastern nationals living in Northern Virginia',[20] the

Operation Green Quest task force, comprising the US Customs Service, IRS, FBI and Secret Service, disrupted suburban equanimity as agents 'broke doors and locks, brandished guns, and used handcuffs while they ransacked homes and offices'.[21]

A subversive community of co-conspirators had allegedly exploited sprawl's unruly dislocations, infiltrating Fairfax County's heterogeneous mix of mandarin power and common democratic culture, tainting the suburban refuge of manicured lawns, asphalt driveways and culs-de-sac that are home to a population of over a million.

The raids, and those that followed, signalled that Northern Virginia's swathe of Greater Washington DC sprawl – a rapidly evolving region shaped by the competing interests of home owners, regional planners, developers, highway engineers and environmentalists – was being remapped under the new geography of national security threat. As they tracked allegedly illicit financial practices, federal agents plotted the contours of an improbable new battlefield along snarled transportation corridors and layers of impervious asphalt that had supplanted the region's wildlife habitats and agricultural greenfields.

Threatscape

Unfolding beyond the historic city's boundaries, Greater Washington – home to one of the nation's largest Muslim populations[22] – had been cast as a distinctive locus of 'homeland', the emerging nationalist project that is reclassifying civilian landscapes as threatscape's defensible space.

With shrewd nomenclature, homeland taxonomies idealise national landscapes to enlist public support for a campaign to design a geography of threat. Landscapes nostalgically extolled in 'land of the free, and home of the brave' support uncritical narratives of national origin, unity, continuity and destiny. In their

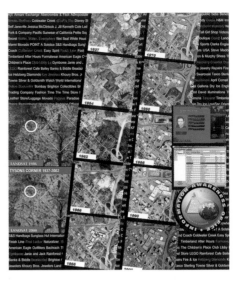

Declassified federal search warrants use the stock vocabulary of the suburban realtor to describe quotidian architectural features of targets of the Herndon raids of March 2002.

The distribution of mosques and Islamic centres reflects Northern Virginia's status as one of the nation's largest Muslim communities. Federal raids on the zone's individuals and institutions suggest the criminalisation of this ethnic geography.

Emerging consumer and car culture supported the growth of Tysons Corner as a dense edge-city. The node is also a dense information space where consumer behaviour is documented in databases that – under the USA Patriot Act – may be examined during government counter-terror investigations.

invasive sweeps across Fairfax and Loudoun County sprawl, the authorities were constructing an incipient homeland cartography.

Homeland invokes both moral order and the spatial conditions of suburban settlement. The iconic diagram of home set within the land betrays the culture's predilection for pastoral rather than urban exemplars, privileging green lawns over city sidewalks. With most of Americans residing in suburbs,[23] threats against this dominant environment command the public's attention as well as its acquiescence to government interventions.

Information Battlespace

During the Civil War, the Defenses of Washington (1862) – a circumferential ring of fortified installations – successfully safeguarded the vulnerable city. Since 11 September, 'next-generation' technologies are administering sprawl's unrestrained landscapes. Streets, sidewalks and back yards that shape the suburban imagination are being reimaged in military-grade surveillance and satellite-based GPS. Constructed in real- and near-real time, sprawl's unpredictable legacy of subdivisions, culs-de-sac, big-box retailers, parking lots, fast-food franchises and high-tech corridors are being reconceptualised as 'battlespace',[24] the multidimensional battlefield constructed by sensor and reporting technologies that conduct intelligence collection, surveillance and reconnaissance. Reconstituted in GIS scene-mapping and mission-planning software,[25] suburban sanctuaries are captive to command-and-control arsenals that have supplanted the omniscient bird's-eye overview.

New technologies reveal latent infrastructures of political control already embedded in suburban landscapes. They expose consumer-driven sprawl as uniquely manipulable information space. The single-family home is a rich lode of sensitive information about debt, cars, credit cards, banking, taxes, travel, school performance and medical history. Data mining's invasive pattern-recognition algorithms – developed from statistics, artificial intelligence and machine learning – scour massive databases on behalf of the government, seeking 'interesting

knowledge'.[26] Sprawl's complex information space has become captive to panoptic schemes of 'multiple cartographies of surveillance'.[27]

Next-Generation Sprawl

National security expansion continues to shape Greater Washington DC sprawl. Stringent new security regulations adopted after 11 September – including 82-foot building set-backs as a precaution against truck bombs – will require as many as 50,000 Department of Defense personnel currently occupying some 8 million square feet of rented space in 140 Northern Virginia buildings to relocate to secure sites in outer suburbs beyond the Beltway.[28] Defence contractors are expected to follow, a migration that could 'exacerbate the region's traffic, destabilize the real estate market and flood already crowded schools'[29] and 'increase suburban sprawl and frustrate "smart growth" efforts in urban areas'.[30]

As sprawl landscapes are hardened behind barbed-wired buffer zones and government transparency is reduced by dark tinted windows, the encroachment of the national security domain – often under cloak of secrecy – has consequences for civilian space and civil liberties. Information activists are harnessing new technologies to educate the public and reverse-engineer the panopticon effect.

Web-based initiatives such as Cryptome (www.cryptome.org), GlobalSecurity (www.globalsecurity.org), the National Security Archive (www.gwu.edu/~nsarchiv/), the Federation of American Scientists (www.fas.org) and Memory Hole (www.thememoryhole.org), as well as online discussion forums, function as national security watchdogs. They offer powerful tools for public education – often in the face of government opposition. Information transparency is empowering the public with critical bird's-eye views of the homeland's contested battlespace. Δ

Notes

1 Vera Cohn and Michael Laris, 'Metro Area Population Continues Upward Trend: Loudoun County Among Nation's Fastest Growing According to Census', *Washington Post*, 15 April 2005, A01; see www.washingtonpost.com/wp-dyn/articles/A52779-2005Apr14.html.
2 *The National Commission on Terrorist Attacks Upon the United States: The 911 Commission Report*, Government Printing Office (Washington DC), 2004, pp 2–35; see www.9-11commission.gov/report/911Report.pdf.
3 'Senate Amendment No 2502: To Withold Funds Allocated for Construction of the Headquarters Buildings of the National Reconnaissance Office,' Congressional Record, 10 August 1994; see www.fas.org/irp/congress/1994_cr/s940810-dod-nro.htm.
4 Cassidy & Pinkard is the area's largest locally owned commercial real-estate firm: 'Cassidy & Pinkard Arranges Sale of Corporate Point III in Westfields', www.cassidypinkard.com/wmspage.cfm?parm1=4365.
5 National Reconnaissance Office, 'Corona', www.nro.gov/corona/facts.html.
6 US Centennial of Flight Commission, 'Balloons in the American Civil War', www.centennialofflight.gov/essay/Lighter_than_air/Civil_War_balloons/LTA5.htm.
7 Steve Vogel, 'Military Has High Hopes for New Eye in the Sky: Sensor-Equipped Blimps Could Aid Homeland Security', *Washington Post*, 8 August 2003, B01.
8 Department of Defense Directorate for Information Operations and Reports, '100 Companies Receiving the Largest Dollar Volume of Prime Contract Awards: Fiscal Year 2001', www.dior.whs.mil/peidhome/procstat/p01/fy2001/top100.htm.
9 Atlee E Shidler (ed), *Greater Washington in 1980: A State of the Region Report,* The Greater Washington Research Center (Washington DC), 1980, pp 6–9.
10 Martin Kady and Mike Sunnucks, '"Bandits" Bank on Bush: Federal Contractors Pin Hopes on Defense Boost', *Washington Business Journal*, 1 June 2001; see www.bizjournals.com/washington/stories/2001/06/04/story1.html.
11 Greater Washington Initiative, 'Get Regional Facts', www.greaterwashington.org/regional/quick_facts/index.htm.
12 Joel Garreau, *Edge City: Life on the New Frontier*, Anchor Press (New York), 1992, pp 6–7.
13 Brent Stringfellow, 'Personal city: Tysons Corner and the question of identity', in A Bingaman, L Sanders and R Zorach (eds), *Embodied Utopias: Gender, Social Change, and the Modern Metropolis*, Routledge (New York), 2002, p 174.
14 'Tysons Corner Center: Mall Directory', www.shoptysons.com/searchstore/index.cfm.
15 'US Army Strategic Communications Command Microwave Station, Tysons Corner, VA (Fort Ritchie Site E)', http://coldwar-c4i.net/Site_E/index.html; and 'Warrenton Station B', www.fas.org/irp/facility/warrenton_b.htm.
16 National Capital Planning Commission, *The National Capital Urban Design and Security Plan*, NCPC (Washington DC), October 2002, pp 6–10. National Capital Planning Commission, *Designing for Security in the Nation's Capital: A Report by the Interagency Task Force of the National Capital Planning Commission*, www.ncpc.gov/planning_init/security/DesigningSec.pdf.
17 Maureen Fan, 'Block by Block, Access Denied: Security Just One Reason D.C. Has Moved Beyond L'Enfant', *Washington Post*, 22 August 2004, A01; see www.washingtonpost.com/wp-dyn/articles/A22340-2004Aug21.html.
18 Simson Garfinkel, *Database Nation: The Death of Privacy in the 21st Century*, O'Reilly & Associates, Inc (Sebastopol, CA), 2000, pp 1–12.
19 'In the Matter of Searches Involving 555 Grove Street, Herndon, Virginia, and Related Locations: [Proposed Redacted] Affidavit in Support of Application for Search Warrant', US District Court for the Eastern District of Virginia, Alexandria Division, October 2003, www.usdoj.gov/usao/vae/ArchivePress/OctoberPDFArchive/03/safaaffid102003.pdf.
20 *Ibid*, p 6.
21 Nancy Dunne, 'Attack On Terrorism – US Homefront: US Muslims See Their American Dreams Die', *Financial Times*, 2 May 2002; see http://specials.ft.com/attackonterrorism/FT3P6NEVBZC.html.
22 District of Columbia, Maryland, and Virginia Advisory Committees to the US Commission on Civil Rights, 'Civil Rights Concerns in the Metropolitan Washington, DC Area in the Aftermath of the September 11, 2001, Tragedies: Chapter 2', June 2003, www.usccr.gov/pubs/sac/dc0603/ch2.htm.
23 Dolores Hayden, *Building Suburbia: Green Fields and Urban Growth 1820–2000*, Pantheon (New York), 2003, p 3.
24 National Defense University, Stuart Johnson and Martin Libicki (eds), *Dominant Battlespace Knowledge*, NDU Press Book (Washington DC), 1995.
25 ESRI, GIS for Homeland Security, ESRI White Paper, November 2001, www.esri.com/library/whitepapers/pdfs/homeland_security_wp.pdf.
26 Usama Fayyaad, Gregory Platetsky-Shapiro and Padhraic Smyth, 'From Data Mining to Knowledge Discovery in Databases', American Association of Artificial Intelligence, *AI Magazine* 17, Fall 1996, pp 37–51.
27 Mark Monmonier, *Spying With Maps: Surveillance Technologies and the Future of Privacy*, University of Chicago Press (Chicago and London), 2002, pp 1–16.
28 Spencer S Hsu, 'Defense Jobs in N.Va. At Risk: Many Buildings Fall Short of New Security Standards', *Washington Post*, 10 May 2005, A01; see www.washingtonpost.com/wp-dyn/content/article/2005/05/09/AR2005050901087.html.
29 David Cho, 'Base Plan Undercuts Sprawl Battle: Region's Leaders Criticize Job Shifts', *Washington Post*, 15 May 2005, A01; see www.washingtonpost.com/wp-dyn/content/article/2005/05/14/AR2005051401190.html.
30 Hsu, *op cit*, A01.

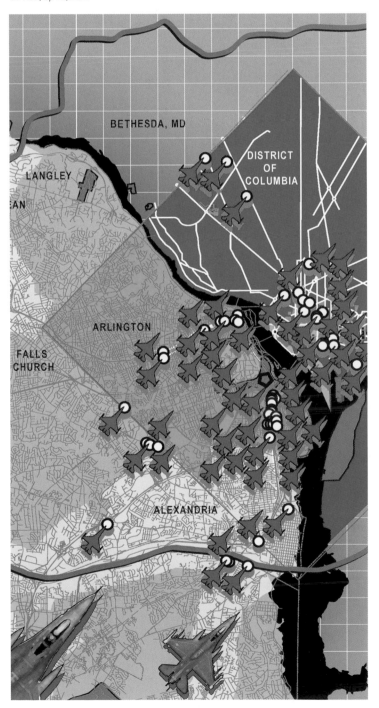

Enlarged detail from top-left illustration on page 82.

Sanjaya loves to drive. He has two GPS navigation systems installed in his car and posts the pictures he takes from the sunroof onto his web site: www.aboutsanjaya.com.

The impact of new technologies on the perception of territory is an old phenomenon. If in modernity it began with transportation infrastructure, with first the train and then the car, we are now facing the introduction of complex electronic networks and remote sensing. Sanjaya's case is particularly interesting since it illustrates both aspects: 20th-century car touring and the new communications infrastructure paradigm. For instance, he makes use of GPS to travel by car through the landscape and, afterwards, uses the World Wide Web to share his experience collectively.

Sanjaya uses the car to escape the city, in his case Washington DC. But the differences between the countryside and urban areas are increasingly fading. In this driving landscape, nature has to be different, yet as comfortable and manageable as the built environment. Furthermore, technology not only preserves and facilitates his access to the natural scenery, but mediates between Sanjaya, his real-time experience and us, his audience. Sanjaya may escape the city, but he does not leave the asphalt.

Technology has been altering some of the basic components of our landscape, such as its naturalness and accessibility. However, although the car and the satellite have modified our perception of the environment, nothing is conclusive. With two GPS receivers on board, Sanjaya still manages to get lost from time to time.

Sanjaya first set up a personal web site in 1993 when the Internet was first becoming popular. On the site, he explains: 'There are many things I like to do, apart from computers and my fascination with technology. Two of the greatest passions of my life are dancing and organising cultural events in Washington DC.'

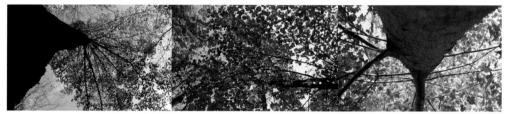

Technology facilitates and, at the same time, frames Sanjaya's relationship with nature. Pictures taken on a trip to Shenandoah National Park, Virginia, 22 October 2000.

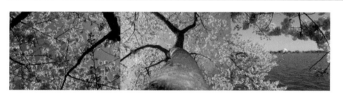

Washington DC and its surrounding areas are mostly depicted as a dynamic and continuous landscape of pleasant drives. 'It usually takes about an hour to go to the Belvedere Hotel from Washington DC, but the drive is worth the effort. If I have time to spare, I usually take the Baltimore Washington Parkway up to Baltimore and enjoy the scenic view of trees along the parkway.'

Technology generates unsuspected connections and usages by operating at different scales. The satellite makes his intimate experience of the landscape available to a large audience which may include, among others, his compatriots back home or the author of this article, in Spain.

Computers and technology have always fascinated Sanjaya. Back in 1997, when his car did not have an on on board GPS navigation system, he was already using a laptop and an external GPS receiver. He believes 'in what technology can do to improve the quality of lives and society in general'.

The road itself is the final destination and Sanjaya enjoys shooting tranquil landscapes as much as interesting 'road pictures'. During a trip to the Shenandoah National Park in Virginia, in 1999, Sanjaya and his friend took some of these images by sticking the camera out of the sunroof and snapping a picture: 'It took us a few pictures to perfect this, but we ended up taking some interesting pictures.'

The Skyline Drive, a 105-mile extension of the 469-mile Blue Ridge Parkway in Virginia, is Sanjaya's favourite destination: 'I like this place so much that I wanted to have a picture of me and my car there.'

Sanjaya describes mostly his weekend drives to Baltimore, to the beach, or along the Skyline Drive in the Shenandoah National Park.

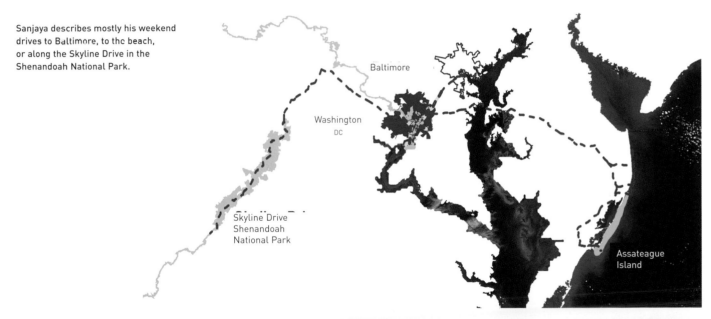

Baltimore

Washington
DC

Skyline Drive
Shenandoah
National Park

Assateague
Island

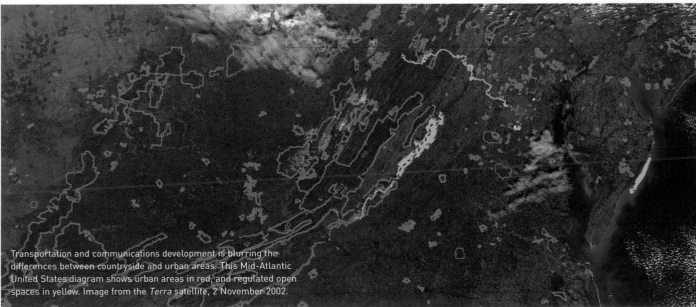

Transportation and communications development is blurring the differences between countryside and urban areas. This Mid-Atlantic United States diagram shows urban areas in red, and regulated open spaces in yellow. Image from the *Terra* satellite, 2 November 2002.

JUST-IN-TIME PLANNING: NEW YORK + HOUSTON

Michael Kwartler counters the rigid determinism of urban planning policy with a just-in-time approach. He describes a new planning, design and regulatory model that harnesses information technologies, such as geographic information systems (GIS) and emerging planning and design-decision support (PDDS), which 'learn' from experience and provide the means to be self-organising and adjusting, responding to rather than anticipating or even trying to direct change.

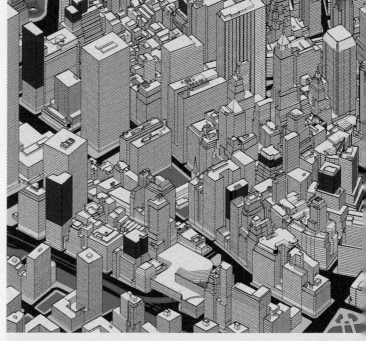

Planning for adaptive reuse in Lower Manhattan using 3-D-GIS
In 1992, the Environmental Simulation Center developed a 3-D-GIS system to examine the adaptive reuse potential of over 25 million square feet of vacant space in office buildings in New York's Lower Manhattan. 3-D-GIS spatially references the database to a floor-by-floor model of every building in Lower Manhattan, thereby enabling the user to capture, query and visualise data on a floor-by-floor basis that made it possible to conceptualise mixing uses at a fine grain, building by building. The database includes zoning, census, infrastructure, building construction and age, floor sizes and total floor area, independent elevator banks and vacancy rates that were updated quarterly. The figures here illustrate a sequential query with the top figure showing all floors above 150 feet that met the criteria for residential reuse, in red; the middle figure showing only those floors in buildings built prior to 1945, in blue; and the bottom figure showing all of the floors in the pre-1945 buildings that were over 50 per cent vacant at that time, in magenta. Beyond the individual building, the 3D-GIS made it possible to understand the probability of adaptive reuse in an area, and whether the aggregate of the floors converted to residential use achieved a critical mass for services and subway stations to be opened at night.

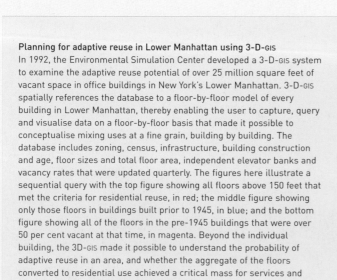

Planners and architects pride themselves on their (mistaken) belief that they can create regulatory regimes that reflect with certainty how citizens will live, work and recreate in the foreseeable future. The result has been highly prescriptive regulations, such as New Urbanist codes, that predetermine, on a site-by-site basis, where activities will happen, the intensity or density of the activities, and overdetermined building form regulations.

This approach to city design defies common sense when the perception, if not the reality, of cities is that they are chaotic and unpredictable entities. In other words, cities are examples of complex systems that manifest self-organising and self-adjusting characteristics. As Kevin Lynch has noted:

[the city] is the product of many builders who are constantly modifying the structure for reasons of their own. While it may be stable in general outlines for sometime, it is ever changing in detail. Only partial control can be exercised over its growth and form. There is no final result, only a continuous succession of phases.[1]

If Lynch's observation is true – and everyday experience tends to bear it out – then the current practice of planning, designing and regulating our cities is distinctly 19th century, where the factory system is applied to city design. In this system, cities are atomised into their component parts, optimised and reassembled into a rationalised whole.

More recently we have begun to see planning, design and regulatory approaches that are decidedly more 21st century: approaches to city planning and design and regulation that are dynamic, that embrace complexity and change, and deal with flows

3-D-GIS of Lower Manhattan illustrating the information, query, and display capabilities of the database
The top two displays are quadrant axonometric views of the 3-D model. Top left displays all the buildings constructed between 1916 – when New York City adopted zoning – and 1945. Top right displays the degree to which all the buildings in Lower Manhattan are either overbuilt, underbuilt or built-out under current zoning, and is used to identify 'soft' or potential redevelopment sites and assemblages by the degree that the site(s) is underbuilt. Bottom left displays a Nolli-type figure-ground planimetric map with buildings shown in black and the spaces between them in white (the Nolli figure-ground map of Rome dates from the late 17th century and was one of the first of its kind to show accurate spatial relationships). The same device is used here to understand the 3-D spatial relationship of buildings in a high-rise district by literally slicing through buildings in 100-foot increments up to heights exceeding 1,000 feet. This display shows buildings and the space around them (including the roofs of lower buildings) at 200 feet. Bottom right displays a composite view showing an aerial perspective of Lower Manhattan and a single block, shown in the insets as an axonometric view and a portion of the block's database.

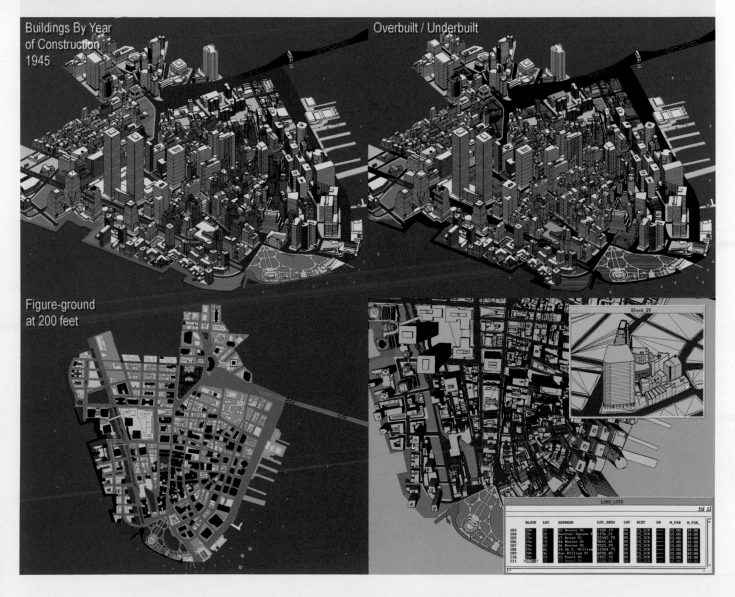

Buildings By Year of Construction 1945

Overbuilt / Underbuilt

Figure-ground at 200 feet

Visualisation can be
tied to GIS data ...

... new policies can be proposed ...
... alternative scenarios can be
constructed in three dimensions ...

... the impacts can be
quickly identified ...

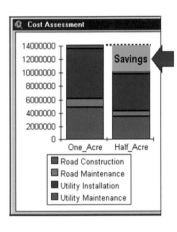

... and everything can
be viewed and modified
instantly in an interactive,
virtual model of the
community.

Community Viz™ planning and design-decision support software
Community Viz™, designed by the Environmental Simulation Center
and its collaborators, is a suite of GIS-based PDDS software designed
for planners, designers and communities that makes all types of
data associated with planning and urban design issues – words,
numbers and images – mutually accountable to each other in an
intuitive, interactive and visual environment that facilitates the
creation, comparison and evaluation of alternative scenarios and strategies. The
process of using Community Viz™ is neither linear nor hierarchical. It has been
designed to encourage the user to simultaneously test and evaluate the
implications of scenarios at different scales, as well as develop and revise all
assumptions, performance indicators and formulae in an accessible, fully
transparent environment.

of information in iterative feedback loops. These feedback loops –
with feedback beginning to occur in real time – make possible a
fundamental change in thinking about planning and regulation,
where demand (bottom-up) rather than supply (top-down) is the
operative principle. Information technology is making these
changes possible. Geographic information systems (GIS), whereby
information is place-based, and emerging planning and design-
decision support (PDDS) software, provide tools that enable cities
and their citizens to be responsive to changing conditions and
demands on how urban space is to be used and configured.

The state of the contemporary city argues for a method of
planning, design and regulation that is 'just-in-time', rather than
'not-in-time' and 'just-in-case', while recognising that some
elements in a city are more stable (for example, infrastructure,
streets, blocks and plots) than others (such as buildings and how
they are used). The metaphor for a Toyota-ist 'just-in-time' system
could be the market. Indeed, Juval Portugali uses the food market
as just such an example:

A miniature of the real big, large-scale case of just-in-

time production and supply systems – the food market of
large cities where a large number of firms of all sizes
supply food for millions of people without creating
shortages or surplus ... and what happens in the food
markets is but one facet, indeed a beautiful illustration,
of a more general property of the city as a self-
organizing system.[2]

The key is timely information provided through feedback
loops. This information is the 21st century's infrastructure
equivalent of the 19th century's water supply systems and
the 20th century's road and communications systems.

The planning, design and regulatory paradigm described
here takes advantage of the accelerating feedback loops
provided by GIS and PDDS, where information feedback on
what is happening on the ground would be evaluated against
expectation of performance. With the aid of GIS, performance
becomes place-based, and plays a critical role in locating
common ground. As Donald Appleyard has observed:

(T)echnical planning and environmental decisions are

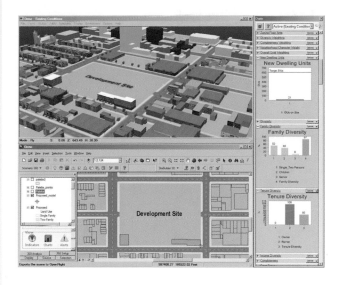

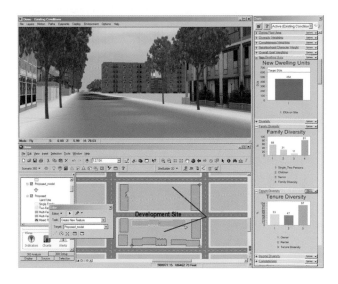

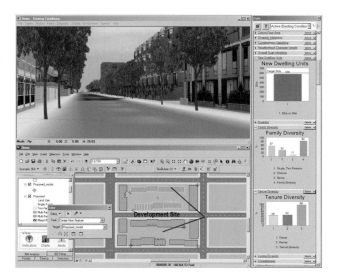

Technologically facilitated community-planning workshop
This series of images is taken from a community-planning
workshop that used Community Viz™. The focus of the workshop
was the urban regeneration of an obsolete industrial area. The
workshop had three components: (1) formulation by the
participants of indicators, bench marks and capacities that would
be used to evaluate the performance of alternative urban-
regeneration scenarios (right-hand columns of the user
interfaces); (2) the development of a 3-D tool box of smart,
attributed neighbourhood 'building blocks'; (3) the design of
alternative urban-regeneration scenarios in real time (lower map
with dynamic view cone and above it the view of the interactive 3-D
model at eye level). The sequence illustrates 'learning by doing',
whereby the participants design a scenario in 3-D by selecting and
placing the smart buildings in the model. Simultaneously, as the
smart building blocks are placed in the 3-D model, the scenario's
performance is evaluated against the indicators, which change as
building blocks are added or subtracted, giving the designers
immediate feedback on the implications of their decisions.

not only value-based ... but identity-based ... (P)hysical
planning decisions can, and frequently do, threaten the
identity and status of certain groups while enlarging the
powers of others.[3]

Performance indicators would be based on commonly
held group values that by their nature are guiding
principles and, hence, have a longer shelf life than the
premeditated 'solutions' often embodied in plans and
regulations, even including the more recent New Urbanist
codes. Performance indicators are measurable using either
qualitative or quantitative variables. An example of a
performance indicator might be 'diversity' and might be
measured by tenure, household income, age of the
householder, along with other variables.

Unlike static systems, this new planning, design and
regulatory paradigm 'learns' from experience and provides
the means to be self-organising and self-adjusting, often
resulting in a 'good' that could not have been anticipated in
a top-down system. A metaphor would be the process in

which moribund 19th- and early 20th-century industrial loft
buildings and districts in Manhattan were illegally converted to
live/work accommodation by artists and others. Facilitated by the
fact that loft buildings are underdetermined and 'loose fit', Lynch's
'builders' experimented with ways to adapt such lofts to the needs
of living and working. This 'group learning' led to the development
of a new housing type, the repositioning of industrial districts and
lofts in the public's mind 20 years later as highly desirable places
to live and work and, ultimately, their legalisation in the city's
zoning resolution.

Based on this example, we can imagine a city design and
regulatory system that encourages creativity – 'the good you can't
think of' – by framing the problem to be solved, rather than
prescribing the solution. For instance, a principle that guides
design and regulatory decision making might be: encourage a
diversity of ways to live and work that do not threaten the well-
being of the inhabitants and their neighbours. The performance of
proposed uses against this principle can be measured by
indicators of performance. By definition performance assumes

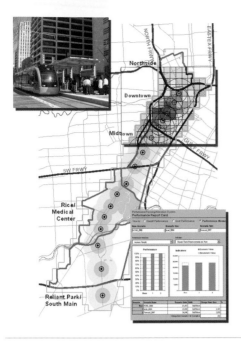

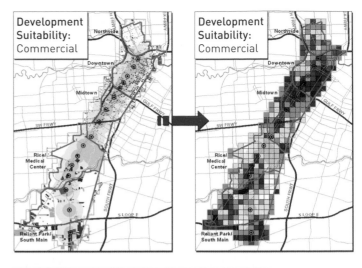

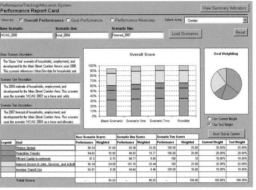

Managing change along Houston's light-rail corridor

Developed for the City of Houston by the Environmental Simulation Center, the Performance/Tracking/Allocation (P/T/A) system monitors growth along the city's recently completed Main Street light-rail corridor. The goals were: (1) measure the performance of the corridor against 22 community-based indicators; (2) track change as it occurs; and (3) allocate future-year growth to where it is likely to occur. It consists of two components: the Land Development Model and the Performance Report Card. The Land Development Model produces its monthly estimates of population, housing units, households and employment by utilising digital information already recorded by the city in the form of building permits. Outputs from the Land Development Model allow the user to examine change for dozens of indicators. In the example opposite, the user can see the spatial distribution of building permits indicating higher than predicted housing activity, and the adjusted forecast. The short feedback loop is extremely useful in targeting the planning and allocation of resources for infrastructure improvements to complement and encourage private investment. The top-right example illustrates the suitability of commercial development at a parcel level based on frontage on busy streets, proximity to light rail, plot size and surrounding uses. The Land Development Model is linked to the Performance Report Card (above), which organises and evaluates the corridor's performance against expectations. Because the districts through which the light rail runs are quite diverse, each district may weight the indicators differently based on community values. Further, the interface allows the user to evaluate performance at multiple levels of geography – the entire corridor, any district or any light-rail station. Both the Land Development Model and Performance Report Card are completely transparent and adjustable by the user.

that there are multiple right answers to a design or planning problem and the degree of 'fit' (see Christopher Alexander's *Notes on the Syntheses of Form*)[4] is the measure of performance.

We can design software built on a GIS platform that incorporates the tools needed to support a just-in-time performance-based planning, design and regulatory regime. PDDS demystifies the intricate process of planning by recognising that words, numbers and images are all ways of representing the world around us. This premise allows us to create 'what-if' scenarios integrating impact analysis (a moment in time), performance evaluation and forecasting (change over time) in an interactive 3-D/virtual reality environment. These tools are designed to support both deductive (analytical) and inductive (intuitive) reasoning in a nonhierarchical, nonlinear structure that supports the way we think.

Most PDDS systems come with no data or formulae. Rather, they are empty shells that need to be populated with information about the community, by the community. The process of using PDDS does not require a specific entry point or order in which its component modules are used. For example, the user is not required to enter at the macroscale of public policy and work towards the micro-scale of neighbourhood block. Instead, the systems encourage the user to simultaneously test and evaluate the implications of a scenario at different scales, modify them on the fly, all in an iterative and interactive process that informs choices.

The principles and performance indicators described above must be formulated and weighted by citizens to ensure that they represent the community's values and sense of identity. This is a critical component of PDDS because it brings citizens together to determine the basis on which they will evaluate events, propositions and proposals, and make choices that are accountable to a shared set of values. A significant outcome of this activity is the creation of social capital.

The best PDDS systems allow everyone to participate in the process – even those who cannot draw or build models. For most citizens, the quality of the place is important, as it is what they experience. PDDS systems such as Community Viz™ enable citizens to approach issues experientially by testing ideas in three dimensions dynamically, greatly enhancing participation and levels of the playing field. In this modality, design itself becomes a form of enquiry.

Unlike conventional planning and regulation, which is episodic (for example, the plan and regulations are done once every 'x' years and then take on a 'mosaic' immutable quality), PDDS would be fully integrated into the public decision-making process to create scenarios, evaluate alternatives and provide the basis for informed public discussion and decision making. In communities, or even neighbourhoods, it is not unusual for the aggregates of incremental decisions, made over time, to lead to unintended and often unwanted consequences. PDDS can

P/T/A system: tracking change and allocating growth

The P/T/A system uses building permits to track change as it occurs and to adjust forecasted growth.

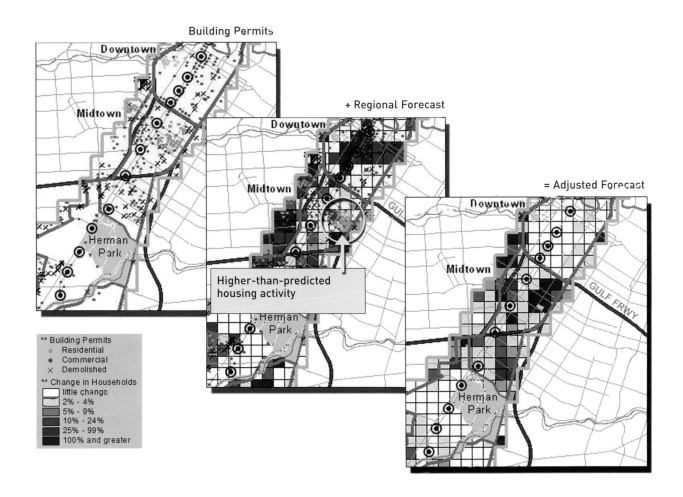

Building Permits

+ Regional Forecast

= Adjusted Forecast

Higher-than-predicted housing activity

** Building Permits
● Residential
● Commercial
✕ Demolished

** Change in Households
little change
2% - 4%
5% - 9%
10% - 24%
25% - 99%
100% and greater

provide the forecasting environment that can suggest where the aggregation of incremental decisions may lead. For example, if we continue 'business-as-usual', what are the short-, medium- and long-term consequences of our actions, and are they acceptable based on our commonly held values and identity? Further, PDDS provides the environment in which to calibrate values and, when necessary, re-evaluate their relevance and their relative and absolute importance based on feedback from prior decisions and actions. A 'good thing' one day might be a 'bad thing' the next day and vice versa. An example of this could be the Eiffel Tower which, when it was built, was widely panned by artists and intellectuals, and only later became a structure revered by Parisians and an icon of the city.

Such tools have the potential to provide the substantive basis for decisions made at the appropriate level, decentralising decision making to those most familiar with the place, the issues and the information needed to inform the decision-making process. The metasystem of commonly held values, principles and performance indicators would be adjusted to local conditions. For example, the performance indicator that evaluates compliance with the diversity principle used above could be weighted differently among all the performance indicators, and the diversity 'mix' adjusted to local goals. The process of localising principles and performance indicators to a

community is critical to the objective of building social capital through a reinvigorated concept of citizenship, and rejects the 'one-size-fits-all' approach to planning, design and regulation.

Finally, the devolution of control made possible by information technology helps to loosen the tight reins of overdetermined systems of control and exclusion into an underdetermined system of inclusion that harnesses responsible individual action and creativity, and sustains the creation of social capital and democratic values. Given the vested interests in the status quo at the national, and even the state, level the local level presents the ideal environment for creativity and democratic decision making based on inclusion and enlightened understanding, control of the agenda, effective participation, and voting equality at the decisive stage.[5] We should seize the moment. ⚏

Notes
1 Kevin Lynch, *Image of the City*, MIT Press (Cambridge, MA), 1960, p 2.
2 Juval Portugali, *Self Organization and the City*, Springer Verlag (Berlin Heidelberg, Germany), 2000, p 36.
3 Donald Appleyard, 'The Environment as Social Symbol', *Journal of the American Institute of Planners* 143, 1979.
4 Christopher Alexander, *Notes on the Synthesis of Form*, Harvard University Press (Cambridge, MA), 1966.
5 Robert A Dahl, *Democracy and Its Critics*, Yale University Press (New Haven, CT and London), 1989.

Native Americans called Long Island Paumonauk, or 'fish-shaped island'. Twenty thousand years ago, recessional deposits of the Wisconsinian glacier created its permeable top layer. Underneath, the melting glacier entrusted great wealth: a crystal lens of pure water held in stasis by raritan clay below and the pressure of surrounding salt water. The Magothy aquifer is replenished only by rain percolating into its localised aquicludes.[1] Like earth, Long Island is a closed hydrogeological system. It is a living laboratory where we could find hope for humane urbanism or presage of difficult times to come.

People have introduced hostile ecologies to this body of land. Rapidly settled in the mid-20th century as a bedroom community to New York City, Long Island is a mature suburb. The savings of its ageing population, once invested in land, now provide sustenance for rampant, continual development. Financing mechanisms pulverise the island into bits of speculative profit that lure people unwittingly to participate in the destruction of their habitat.[2] Built with federal funds and underwritten by the price of oil, expressways are enlarged to feed evolving species of sprawl. In the centre of the island, drainage routes to the cavity-riven Magothy, smothered by suburban viscera and contaminated by postindustrial secretions (runoff from parking lots, road salts and radioactive plumes), become hidden pockets of death.

On Long Island, an emerging terrain of mobile electro-communications and digital information technology challenges this alien landscape.

Notes

1 An aquifer is a water-bearing rock. An aquiclude is a body of water that can occur in between impermeable rock. My layperson's understanding of the structure of the Magothy is that it is an aquifer with intermittent aquicludes.
2 Michele Bertomen, 'Commodification of Land', unpublished paper, 2004.

Section through Long Island showing simplified aquifer strata
The Magothy aquifer is replenished solely by rainfall, primarily from the central spine of the island. Water taken from the Magothy must be replaced to maintain hydrostatic pressure so as to prevent salt-water intrusion. This is a global problem, even deep inland.

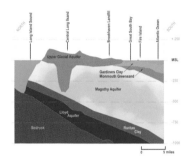

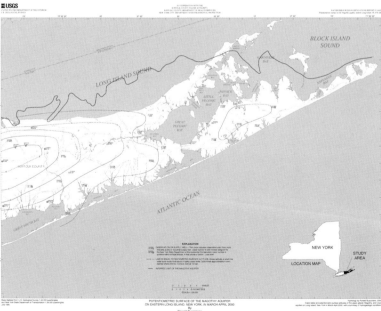

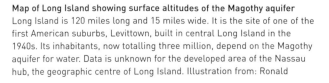

Map of Long Island showing surface altitudes of the Magothy aquifer
Long Island is 120 miles long and 15 miles wide. It is the site of one of the first American suburbs, Levittown, built in central Long Island in the 1940s. Its inhabitants, now totalling three million, depend on the Magothy aquifer for water. Data is unknown for the developed area of the Nassau hub, the geographic centre of Long Island. Illustration from: Ronald Busciolano, *Water-Table and Potentiometric-Surface Altitudes of the Upper Glacial, Magothy, and Lloyd Aquifers on Long Island, New York, in March–April 2000*, US Geological Survey, Water Resources Investigation Report 01-4165, plates 2a,b.

Engaging the new terrain

Long Islander David Schieren in his Prius, using a mobile phone with Blue Tooth technology and a global-positioning system to engage the new terrain in time of his making. Permeable strata in the digital landscape offer alternative routes to comprehend/conquer this emerging territory.

Representational collage of an emerging landscape of mobility and digital communications

Patterns of electrocommunications overlay vehicular routes. The convergence of wireless communications and mobility creates new terrain and perceived space, the geography and boundaries of which have yet to be explored. Does this new realm hold hope for Long Island's future?

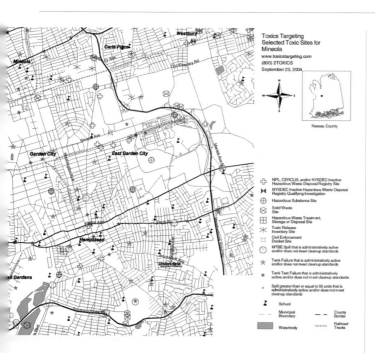

Documented incidents of pollution in the Nassau hub as reported to the New York State Department of Environmental Conservation

Maps of potential pollution sites are rapidly being disseminated via the Internet, as are maps and documentation of the history of land use and ownership. Illustration from www.toxicstargeting.com, composited by Michele Bertomen.

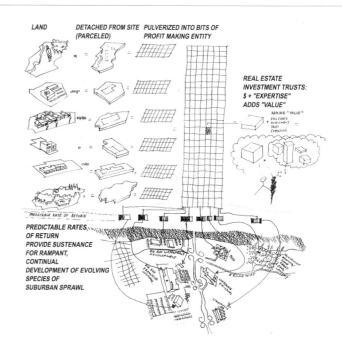

Pulverisation of land into speculative bits of profit via financing and value-adding strategies of a typical real-estate investment trust

The invisibility of these tactics allows Long Islanders to participate unwittingly in the destruction of their land. However, the complex relationships between land use, capital flows and survival are increasingly evident to Long Islanders who have the means to make full use of digital information and communications technology.

Contributor Biographies

Michael Batty is Bartlett Professor of Planning and directs the Centre for Advanced Spatial Analysis (CASA) at University College London. His recent research has been on building mathematical models of cities using complexity theory, as reflected in his book *Cities and Complexity: Understanding Cities Through Cellular Automata, Agent-Based Models, and Fractals* (MIT Press, 2005). He is also editor of the journal *Environment and Planning B*.

Kadambari Baxi is a partner with Martin/Baxi Architects, an ideas-based practice in New York engaged simultaneously in commissioned work and design research. She is also a principal of imageMachine, a new media design practice specialising in work for nonprofit organisations. She is a co-author (with Reinhold Martin) of *Entropia* (Black Dog Publishing, 2001). Martin/Baxi is currently working on another publication entitled *Multi-National Cities: Architectural Itineraries*.

Michele Bertomen is an associate professor at the New York Institute of Technology (NYIT) School of Architecture and Design, and a founding member of Brooklyn Architects Collective, PC. She is the author of *Transmission Towers on the Long Island Expressway: A Study of the Language of Form* (Princeton Architectural Press, 1992), and is currently working to reclaim public space at the water's edge in Williamsburg, in Brooklyn.

Elisabeth Blum is an architect who teaches at the Hochschule für Gestaltung und Kunst Zurich. She is a member of the Building Committee, Lucerne, and member of the advisory boards of Forum für Gestaltung Ulm and of the book collection Bauwelt Fundamente. Publications include *Le Corbusiers Wege* (Birkhauser, 2001) and *FavelaMetropolis: Berichte und Projekte aus Rio de Janeiro und São Paulo* (Birkhäuser, 2004), which she co-edited with Peter Neitzke.

Eric Cadora directs the Justice Mapping Center (JMC) at the JFA Institute. He is co-author, with Dr Todd Clear, of the book *Community Justice* (Wadsworth, 2002), which reviews the emergence of community policing in the 1980s, community courts in the 1990s, and the beginnings of new community corrections in 2000.

Alessandro Cimini received his architecture diploma at La Sapienza, Rome, and his MAUD at Columbia University. He is an associate at AQC Architects in New York City, and was a visiting critic at Syracuse University.

Elie Derman founded CITYSTUDIO architecture in 2001 with Els Verbakel. They are currently practising in Belgium, Israel and New York. Derman is an architect and urban designer from Israel. He teaches architectural design at the Pratt School of Architecture and New Jersey School of Architecture. His design research focuses on borders between the human and the natural. He has won several awards for excellence in design and his work has been exhibited internationally.

Keller Easterling is an architect, urbanist and writer. Her forthcoming book, *Enduring Innocence: Global Architecture and its Political Masquerades* (MIT Press, 2005), researches familiar spatial products that have landed in difficult or hyperbolic political situations around the world. Her most recent book, *Organization Space: Landscapes, Highways and Houses in America* (MIT Press, 1999) applies network theory to a discussion of American infrastructure and development formats.

Rodrigo Guardia teaches an urban design studio at Konkuk University in Seoul. He has lived in Panama City (BArch University of Panama) and New York (MSAUD Columbia University), practising architecture and participating in publications, exhibitions, lectures and critiques. He was part of the Arté New York team that won first prize for the New York New Housing competition, Queens site.

Dr Andrew Hudson-Smith is a systems administrator and lecturer at the Centre for Advanced Spatial Analysis (CASA) at University College London, where he directs the Virtual London project. His research is on multimedia and virtual worlds using avatars in virtual design studios and exhibition spaces, as reflected in his paper '30 Days in ActiveWorlds: Community, Design and Terrorism in a Virtual World', which was published in *The Social Life of Avatars, Presence and Interaction in Shared Virtual Environments* (Springer-Verlag, 2001).

Mark Isarangkun na Ayuthaya is a practising architect and a full-time faculty member at the Faculty of Architecture, Chulalongkorn University, Bangkok. He received a Master of Science in Urbanism from Delft University of Technology, the Netherlands, in 2004, and a Master of Architecture from Chulalongkorn University in 2002.

May Joseph is director of the programme in critical and visual studies and an associate professor of global studies at Pratt Institute, New York. She has written widely on urbanism, performance and visual culture, and is the author of *Nomadic Identities: The Performance of Citizenship* (University of Minnesota Press, 1999) and co-editor of *Performing Hybridity* (Minnesota, 1999). Other edited volumes include *New Hybrid Identities* and *Bodywork* (Women and Performance, 1995 and 1999).

Krystina Kaza received a degree in international relations from James Madison College in 1992, and received a BArch from the Cooper Union in 2003. In 2003/04 she received a Fulbright grant to study Balkrishna Doshi's Aranya Community Housing in Indore, India. She currently teaches and practises in Auckland, New Zealand. She would like to thank Ms Revati Ekbote, Mr Vijay Gangani and Professor MK Chauhan, whose assistance made her research possible.

Hans Kiib is a professor at Aarlborg University. He received his MA in architecture from the Århus School of Architecture in 1977, and his PhD in 1987 from Aalborg University. From 1988 to 1997 he was an associate professor in urban planning at Aalborg, where he founded the School of Architecture and Design, acting as head of the school from 1997 to 2005. His main research interest is related to urban architecture and design, focusing on the welfare city development.

Laura Kurgan teaches architecture at Columbia University. She is director of visual studies and of the new Spatial Information Design Lab. She is currently collaborating with the Justice Mapping Center (directed by Eric Cadora). Her work, which has been exhibited internationally, is collected in *You Are Here: Post-Military Technology and the New Landscape of Satellite Images* (MIT Press, forthcoming).

Michael Kwartler, FAIA is an architect, planner, urban designer and educator. He is the founding director of the Environmental Simulation Center, a nonprofit research laboratory created to develop innovative applications of information technology for community planning, design and decision making. His professional practice and teaching has focused on urban design and the theory and practice of legislating aesthetics/good city form.

Ignacio Lamar received his architecture diploma at the school of architecture, Universidad Central de Venezuela, in Caracas, and his MAUD and MAAD at Columbia University. He is an associate at AQC Architects in New York City, and was a visiting critic at Columbia University and Syracuse University.

Jan Leenknegt holds degrees in architectural engineering (KULeuven, Belgium) and in urban design (Columbia University). Recent design collaborations include a new town in China, public spaces in Europe, a house in Lebanon, a winning proposal for the 2004 New York New Housing competition, and a restaurant tower in Tokyo. He currently lives in New York.

José Luis Echeverría Manau qualified as an architect at the ETSAB (2000) and Columbia University (2002). He has been academic director of the Institute of Advanced Architecture of Catalunya (IaaC). In 2004 he founded 111 together with Jordi Mansilla Ortoneda and Jorge Perea Solano. He currently teaches the first-year design studio at the La Salle School of Architecture in Barcelona.

Gitte Marling received her MA in architecture from the Århus School of Architecture in 1977, and PhD in 1991 from Aalborg University. From 1984 to 1997 she was associate professor in urban ecology and planning at Aalborg, founding the School of Architecture and Design, and is now an associate professor in urban design. Her main research interest is related to urban ecology, urban architecture and public domain.

Victoria Marshall is adjunct assistant professor of architecture at Columbia University where she teaches urban design with a focus on the US Northeast Megalopolis – translating the urban ecosystem approach to urban design models. She is also adjunct assistant professor of landscape architecture at the University of Toronto. Her Hoboken, New Jersey based practice TILL engages water systems and recreation programming with horticultural research.

Brian McGrath is an architect and co-founder of urban-interface.com. He teaches at the Parsons School of Design and Columbia University, where he is co-director of the Urban Field Station, an urban ecology research lab. He was a Senior Fulbright Scholar in Thailand and is currently a co-investigator in the Baltimore Ecosystem Study, where he coordinates a working group studying the links between science and design.

Petia Morozov is an architect and urban designer, and co-founder of madLAB, an interdisciplinary design laboratory exploring creative alliances between design and technology. Her work engages robust urban design models for research and practice, operating within a matrix of scales and disciplines. She also teaches urban design at Columbia University's Graduate School of Architecture Preservation and Planning, with a focus on the US Northeast Megalopolis.

Deborah Natsios is a principal of Natsios Young Architects in New York City. She is co-founder, with John Young, of Cryptome.org and Cartome.org, online archives of 25,000 documents relating to new technologies, national security, geospatial intelligence and civil liberties issues. She has taught architecture and urban design at Columbia University, Parsons School of Design, Pratt Institute and the University of Texas at Arlington.

Peter Neitzke was the architectural editor for the German publisher Friedr Vieweg & Son for more than 20 years. He is the co-editor, with Ulrich Conrads, of the book-collection Bauwelt Fundamente, published by Birkhauser, and founder (1992) and co-editor of *CENTRUM Jahrbuch Architektur und Stadt*, published by Verlag Das Beispiel, Darmstadt. He is also co-editor, with Elisabeth Blum, of *FavelaMetropolis: Berichte und Projekte aus Rio de Janeiro und São Paulo* (Birkhäuser, 2004).

Jordi Mansilla Ortoneda qualified as an architect at the ETSAB in 2000. He has worked for architectural practices such as FOA (London–Tokyo) and Atélier Jean Nouvel (Paris–Barcelona). In 2004 he founded 111 together with Jorge Perea Solano and José Luis Echeverría Manau. He currently teaches the second-year design studio at the La Salle School of Architecture in Barcelona.

Emmanuel Pratt holds a BArch from Cornell University and an MSUAD from Columbia University. His professional work has ranged from corporate web and motion design, broadcast editing and experimental documentary work in both film and mixed media. He is presently based in Johannesburg where he is a visiting lecturer in the architecture department at the University of Witwatersrand.

Antonio Scarponi is an architect who develops conceptual devices as a result of interdisciplinary research projects, involving design, architecture and visual culture, with the aim of engaging practices and social behaviour in everyday life. A conceptual device transforms information into a visual knowledge that produces and shifts symbolic values. He was a visiting student at Cooper Union, and received his MA at IUAV, Venice, where he is currently a PhD researcher.

David Grahame Shane received his Architectural Association diploma in 1969, his MArch in urban design from Cornell University in 1972, and PhD from Cornell in 1978. He teaches urban design at Columbia, lectures on urban design at the Bartlett and participates in urban design master classes at the University of Venice. He also teaches at Cooper Union and City College in New York. Publications include *Recombinant Urbanism: Conceptual Modelling in Architecture, Urban Design and City Theory* (John Wiley & Sons, 2004).

Christopher Small, a geophysicist at the Lamont-Doherty Earth Observatory of Columbia University, received his PhD from the Scripps Institution of Oceanography in 1993. His early experience ranged from shipboard studies of Chesapeake Bay with the University of Maryland, to satellite mapping with the Exxon Production Research Company. Current research interests focus on measuring changes in the earth's surface and understanding the causes and consequences of these changes.

Jorge Perea Solano graduated in architecture from ETSAB in 1998. From 1998 until 2004 he worked with Manuel de Solà-Morales on various urban-scale projects worldwide. In 2004 he founded 111 together with José Luis Echeverría Manau and Jordi Mansilla Ortondea. He is the director of the 'Beyond Utopias' course at the IES-University of Chicago in Barcelona.

Erika Svendsen is a research urban planner for the USDA Forest Service, Northeastern Research Station based in New York City. She serves as the co-director of the Urban Field Station, a mobile urban ecology research lab created in cooperation with Columbia University Graduate School of Architecture Planning and Preservation. Her current work includes developing urbanism and public-health programmes with government agencies and community-based groups throughout the US Northeast Megalopolis.

Manolo F Ufer received his masters in housing and urbanism with distinction from the AA in London (2001), and a Master of Science in architecture and urban design from Columbia University (2004), where he was recipient of the Lucille Smyser Lowenfish Memorial Prize and the William Kinne Fellowship. He is currently based in New York City where he has founded ARCHIPELAGOS.

Els Verbakel founded CITYSTUDIO architecture with Elie Derman in 2001, working in Belgium, Israel and New York. She is an architect and urban designer from Belgium, currently working on her PhD in EU urbanism at Princeton University. She teaches architecture and urban design at Columbia University, the Pratt School of Architecture and New Jersey School of Architecture. She has won multiple awards for her scholarly work and has been published internationally.

Eugènia Vidal graduated in architecture from ETSAB in 1999, and received a Master of Science in architecture and urban design from Columbia University in 2002, sponsored by 'la Caixa' scholarship. After teaching several courses and seminars at Columbia University, the Catholic University of America and Universitiat Politècnica de Catalunya, she is currently establishing an architecture and urban design practice in Barcelona. AD

Gluckman Mayner Architects, One Kenmare Square,
New York City, 2005
The rippling front facade of this boutique apartment building,
by Gluckman Mayner Architects for developer Andre Balazs,
gives little indication of the diversity of spaces inside.

THE
BOUTIQUE
APARTMENT

In New York, the gap between living lofts and boutique hotels is being eclipsed. The organisation of rooms in new apartment blocks is becoming complicated. Craig Kellogg reveals how a brave new world of designer floor plans has begun to introduce a welcome complexity.

Until recently, a New Yorker living in apartment 13H could safely sleepwalk down in 9H (or up in 17H) without bumping into a single unexpected wall. The modern American apartment building was always a stack of identical pancakes, with floor after floor configured similar to – if not exactly the same as – those above and below. Penthouses were lavish and wildly different, of course. But otherwise apartment kitchens were small – usually windowless caves. New York bathrooms were even smaller and just as dark. Bedrooms, though they boasted windows, were also compact. And you would not typically find a home office unless an apartment owner had bothered to convert an extra bedroom. For developers, replicating uninspired layouts ad nauseum was easier than building a lot of one-off apartments. People accepted the designs, if sometimes grudgingly, because New York apartments were something like a commodity – and because people needed places to live.

Perhaps a decade ago, some New York developers switched to building new loft-apartment buildings. Lofts are easy, in a sense, being nothing more than white-painted boxes with raw concrete floors. Everyone understood that the rudimentary plumbing fixtures and kitchen benches installed by developers existed only to satisfy city requirements and then be ripped out. From the buyer's point of view, the loft concept spelled liberation from the tyranny of sameness. Any gratification, however, was maddeningly delayed. The raw lofts were DIY housing, and not everyone wanted to budget time and money to build walls and plumbing – let alone contact an architect and engage a builder – before moving in.

Finishing a loft was nothing like taking a suite at a boutique hotel, where the lights were dimmed and the stereo humming upon check-in. But perhaps it was inevitable that someone would close the gap and make the connection between apartments and hotel design. It's not really a surprise to find hoteliers involved in the housing game. The golden era of boutique projects – inaugurated by celebrity hotelier Ian Schrager and

sustained by Andre Balazs – has ended. Schrager and Balazs are, however, fully invested in the latest trend to emerge: the boutique apartment. Advertised as the work of celebrity designers, the apartments are loft-like yet fully finished. In some cases they may even be delivered fully furnished.

Buildings by Richard Gluckman and John Pawson are nearing completion in New York. Balazs has even switched a forthcoming hotel designed by Jean Nouvel, rejigging it into apartments. But not just any apartments. Expensive apartments. The boutique customer is looking for something distinctive. Pawson-designed units now under construction display more than a few of his fingerprints, right down to the custom cherry-veneer Boffi cabinetry, built according to a minimalist design provided by the architect, so there's not even the slightest indication about which side of the kitchen-cabinet door is hinged and which side swings.

You might think that a name like Pawson's would justify stratospheric prices. The developers were not so sure. According to the conventional wisdom, it's terraces and Roman tubs that really drive sales. (And one assumes that Pawson is not exactly a Roman tub sort of guy.) Enter the consultants to explain who, exactly, wants what; what exactly is wanted; and where to put it. Architects like Ismael Leyva, who has been affiliated with several boutique apartment projects, provide interior layouts for apartments within building shells by more famous peers. It's not glamorous work, but behind the scenes Leyva and other 'real-estate consultants' draft floor plans for the highest profile architect-designed buildings.

In one sense these consultants are the gatekeepers of New York's interiors vernacular. Architects tend to nurture new and sometimes shocking ideas. Buyers, on the other hand, are the voice of bourgeois convention. A local developer such as Balazs is well positioned to stay responsive to local buyers' whims. But as property development becomes increasingly internationalised – with companies like the London-based Yoo entering the picture – consultants such as Leyva ensure saleable layouts packed with the features New Yorkers demand; for example, double wash basins in the master bathroom.

In his capacity as a consultant to the developers, Leyva checks for the wash basins, and locates the

Top John Pawson, 50 Gramercy Park North, New York City, 2005
For New York hotelier-turned-developer Ian Schrager, John Pawson has reimagined an old beige brick building on Gramercy Park as a luxury development of boutique apartments.

Second from top In a digital rendering, one of the Pawson living rooms sports classic blue-chip Modernism, including Hans Wegner armchairs and an architectural redwood sofa by RM Schindler.

Second from bottom The kitchens were made in cherry veneer by the Italian manufacturer Boffi, according to a Pawson design.

Bottom left Many of the Pawson apartments feature terraces, a sure way to attract upper-end buyers.

Bottom right Pawson imbued the apartment interiors, which are being built from scratch, with his signature minimalist detailing.

Boutique Logic

Though it's true that the tide of boutique hotels has ebbed, don't count out Philippe Starck. Not so much a designer as a theatrical promoter, Starck singularly put the boutique concept onto the international style radar. He has continued as an industrial designer, working for the Italian lighting manufacturer Flos. Duravit, his German partner for 10 years in the manufacture of bathroom fittings, recently announced a bridge line of lower-priced Starck-designed porcelain that the company will manufacture abroad, to fight against lower-priced imports. Starck, meanwhile, has also joined the boutique apartment bandwagon, as a partner in British developer Yoo. And, in addition to designing the public spaces for Yoo's recent Wall Street-area loft apartment project, he developed decor for the units. A partnership with the local furniture gallery Moss allowed residents to order everything in advance, so that the units could be completely furnished on move-in day.

Roman tub right where buyers expect it: under a window with a skyline view. But not on every floor. Variety, for the consultants, is the spice of life. So apartment 9H, to return to the opening example, may not have a brother in the building. Hallways in the new Manhattan high-rise apartments are more like streets of tract homes in the suburbs. Every floor of a high-rise, like a swathe of virgin farmland being developed, is now considered a blank slate. One floor may have units planned for sexy singles, and the next host sprawling families. In real-estate terms, it's all forecast in advance. Buyers in the sales office who have picked the layout that suits them can consult a schematic drawing to find their floor.

Confronted with the jumble of layouts inside the building he is doing for Balazs, in downtown Manhattan, Gluckman took the extraordinary measure of creating a facade to reflect the diversity going on within. Though perhaps a bit chaotic for some observers, the effect is utterly fresh. Ganged and grouped, the deeply punched windows trip across the building's skin in a staccato rhythm subtly in concert with the layouts of apartments behind. Δ+

The Pavilion at work.

SERPENTINE GALLERY PAVILION 2005

The Serpentine Gallery Pavilion is a unique programme that commissions architecture for art's sake. It provides innovative architects, who have not previously built in the UK, with the opportunity to design a cutting-edge structure for a summer show. **Jeremy Melvin** describes how Portuguese masters Álvaro Siza and Eduardo Souto de Moura, in collaboration with Cecil Balmond of Arup, have produced 'an urban design' that is perfectly calibrated to respond to its Hyde Park setting.

Despite the apparent incongruity of being housed in a 1930s Neoclassical former teahouse in Hyde Park, the Serpentine Gallery has established itself as one of London's leading contemporary art venues. Since 2000, it has sought to offset its traditional setting with an architecture programme of summer pavilion buildings by architects who, at the time of commissioning, had never completed a new building in the UK – all infused with the structural genius of Arup's Cecil Balmond.

This year's collaboration, between Álvaro Siza and Eduardo Souto de Moura, gives two of continental Europe's most renowned architects an opportunity to capitalise on their popularity in London – when either of them lectures in the city, tickets are like gold dust – with a realised structure, albeit one that will be removed after only a few months. They – and the fate of their pavilion – follow Oscar Niemeyer (2003), Toyo Ito (2002), Daniel Libeskind (2001) and Zaha Hadid, who started the programme in 2000. With another design by MVRDV in development, the Serpentine pavilions have established themselves alongside events such as the Royal Academy's Annual Architecture Lecture as a high point of London architecture's summer season.

Siza's and Souto de Moura's is no exception. As anyone who has followed their work might expect, an apparently simple form turns out to be full of subtle complexities and inflections laden with reference to the site and programme. The setting, between the 1930s building and West Carriage Drive, which cuts through the park, seems to be innocuous. However, in line with the English landscape tradition, nothing is quite what it seems. The gentle folds of the lawn and the placing of a nearby tree are consciously created effects. 'It's an urban building,' says Souto de Moura in response to a question about whether they consider the pavilion an urban or rural building, 'but in a park.'

The architects decided to engage with the *genius loci*, orchestrating a conversation between tree, land and building that, in turn, sets off imaginative interpretations of programme and function. On the facade facing the orthogonal gallery, the pavilion seems to shrink into a concave half-ellipse, creating a small forecourt between the two buildings. The design also gently sculpts away at the ground to create a level base – previous pavilions tended to float above the slightly undulating site – with surplus soil making a slight mound. The presence of the tree also exerted a strong influence, while the existing building established a height line. So despite a very different form and different materials, there is an overall sense of composition that ties the new and old buildings together through a sophisticated appreciation and discreet leavening of their setting – the sort of dialogue they create in their other projects, but very much in the English park ethos.

Siza takes up the story: 'The expression [of the two buildings] is very different, but they are related [at the level of] an idea.' That 'idea', shaped and refined in ongoing discussion – 'it's like playing chess', says Souto de Moura – eventually achieves a composition where, says Siza, 'the relationship [between the elements] is inevitable'. Taking up these influences is a necessary but not sufficient step towards the design; ultimately, for Siza, there has to be an underlying logical coherence.

From the outside, the pavilion's form seems to fit into its topography, as if belonging to the shape of the ground. Inside reveals a different relationship, as the roof appears to rise on its legs – the bottom 1.3 metres is left open, so the ground, apart from changing to the grey brick of the gallery from grass, flows without impediment underneath. This relationship also suits the programme, as the pavilion provides space for evening lectures and a daytime café, functions that the restricted accommodation of the main gallery cannot provide.

The Serpentine pavilions have to be designed and built quickly and economically, constraints that in Siza's and Souto de Moura's construction had a bearing on the choice of timber as the main material. Given the time scale, explains Siza, 'the connecting elements had to be steel or wood'. With the form established through drawings passed between the two architects and Balmond – all three had collaborated before on various projects, including the wonderfully thin 18-metre-span concrete canopy at Lisbon's Expo '98 – Arup developed a computer program that must have been fearsomely complex to describe the shape and, from this, the individual elements could be designed and ultimately fabricated.

Though close in form, each of the laminated veneer lumbar timber components is different, and so, logically, are the openings between them, filled with polycarbonate panels that themselves are studded with 'chimneys'. Where vertical, these chimneys also include solar lights that emit enough light to read for up to four

Top left
The pavilion enters into a dialogue with a nearby tree, and also provides the gallery with facilities for dialogue.

Top right
As an object in the landscape, it enters into a dialogue with the ground and tree line.

Bottom
The interior is light and airy, an effect reinforced by leaving the sides open at low level.

Top left
Planometric view, showing the pavilion form and existing gallery,
and the manipulation of the precinct between them.

Bottom left
One of Arup's models developed to establish the structural form.

Top right
Each piece of timber is different.

Bottom right
Diagram showing the relationship between each piece
of timber and how they join to make a structure.

hours after sundown. The timber members fit together by the very traditional means of mortice and tenon joints, and the perfection of their fit means that steel bolts are unnecessary – though they were apparently useful during erection. As Siza says: 'Everything new has a lot of history in it.'

Technically, explains Balmond, the structure is a reciprocal shell, where every structural member 'lives' off those to which it connects, and these interconnections are vital for stability. The visual effect is arresting as, rather than the straight and smooth lines much loved by architects like Foster, the ribs seem to wander around, not quite aligned but nonetheless describing an overall homogeneous form. There is perhaps a trite analogy between the indirect connections between elements and Siza's interpretation of the influences, though the effect is certainly a sense of unity through complexity. Balmond refers to a shared interest in Arte Povera, using the most basic materials and apparently simple techniques to create a richness of expression through

intellect. Siza and Souto de Moura speak of an interest in the vernacular, but also of how their perceptions of the environment where both grew up in northern Portugal were infused with ideas from outside. Siza, the senior by almost 20 years, specifically cites the influence of Architecture d'Aujourdhui. Infusing the vernacular with an intellectual sophistication – whether developed through drawing, computer programs or both – until it ceases to be vernacular is a hallmark of both architects' work.

This small project indicates a much wider spread of geography and history. The timber comes from Finland and was fabricated in Germany. Design work took place on an axis between London and Oporto, where both architects are based – when not working in Barcelona (Souto de Moura) or a vast 200,000-square-metre hospital in Toledo, Spain (Siza), as well as further afield. But such connections are not new, especially to

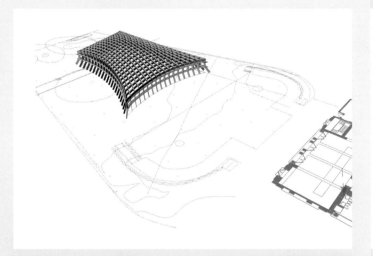

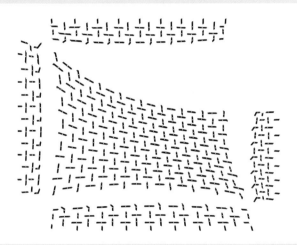

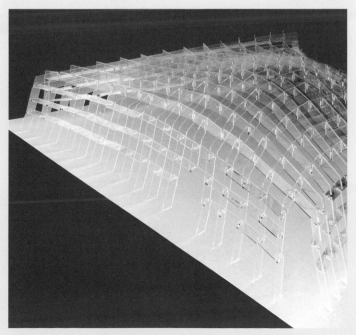

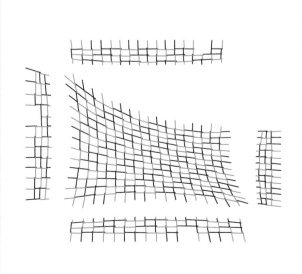

Top left
The actual jointing technology is the traditional mortice and tenon. It is the form that arises from the joints and profiles of the timber that is innovative.

Bottom left
Plan: the building is almost like a rug spread for a picnic in the park, taking shelter from the trees and succour from the existing gallery.

Top left
The actual jointing technology is the traditional mortice and tenon. It is the form that arises from the joints and profiles of the timber that is innovative.

Bottom left
Plan: the building is almost like a rug spread for a picnic in the park, taking shelter from the trees and succour from the existing gallery.

Top, middle and bottom right Three different visions: sketches by Siza (interior view), Souto de Moura (interior view) and Balmond (inter alia overall structural form on the left, and ideas for connections on the right). Even their early sketches are revealing. Siza's encapsulates almost every feature of the completed building, and Souto de Moura's captures the power of the space and, on the bottom right, the essential plan form, while picking up the formal and spatial ideas and representing them in a way that can translate into structure and construction.

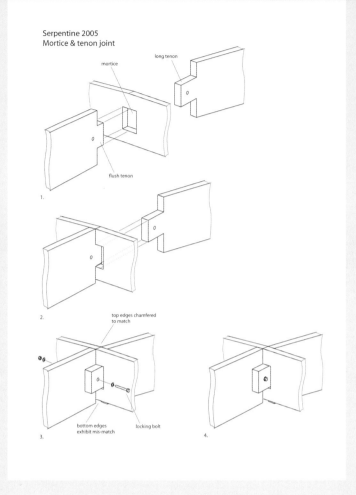

Serpentine 2005
Mortice & tenon joint

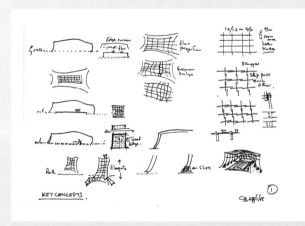

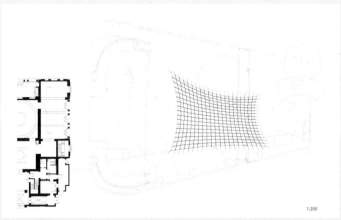

1:200

the Portuguese. Stones used for ballast for ships found their way into churches in Brazil, replaced for the return voyage by gold. Ideas, circulated by travellers or magazines, have always eluded specific localities. 'It's globalisation,' says Souto de Moura.

Given that Siza, Souto de Moura and Balmond collaborate as a trio and in each possible pairing, the relationship is a happy one. Siza enjoys working with engineers. At the Serpentine, he says, engineering 'helped to give scale' to the design, as well as expertise in timber performance. Such support frees him up

to do 'what only the architect can do'. The most important aspect, he continues, is 'coordination' between the various parts: physical, environmental and programmatic. To avoid 'chaos', someone has to have the overall vision, to 'maintain the basic idea, but also to be able to transform it', to synthesise yet transcend the constraints of the various influences. Far from chaotic, the Serpentine Gallery Pavilion is an erudite essay in the subtle complexity of form that comes through such transformations of basic matter and impression. Δ+

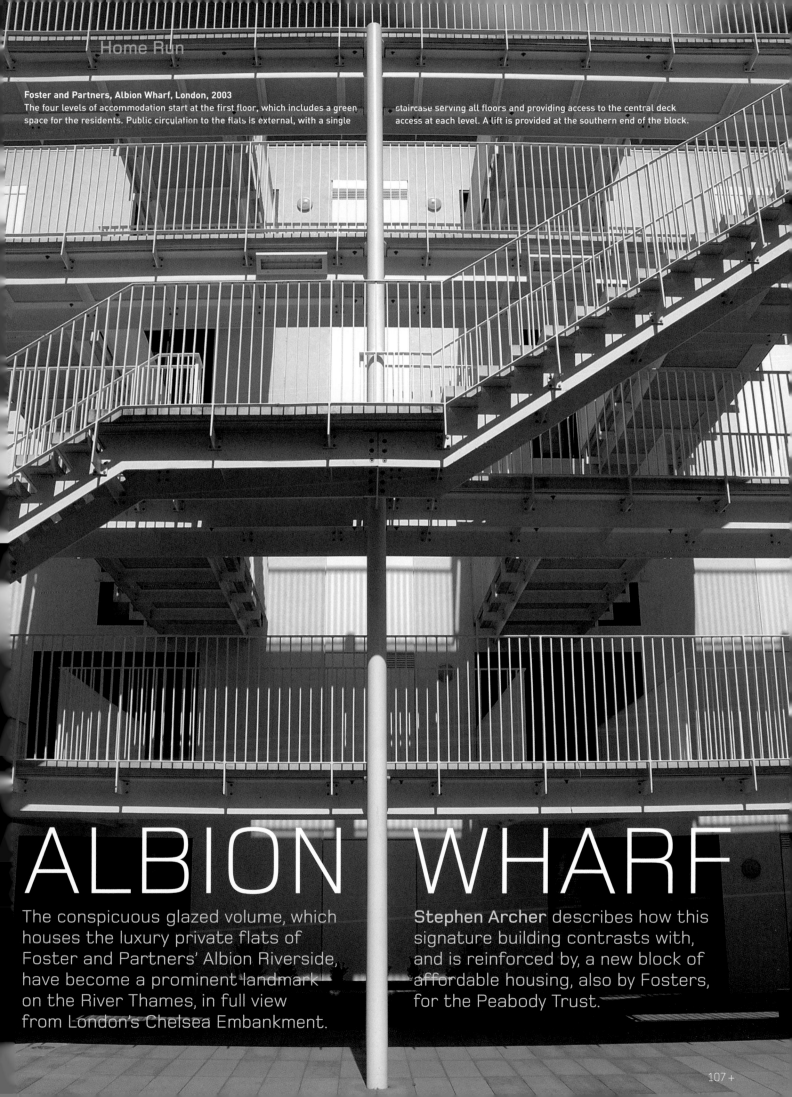

Foster and Partners, Albion Wharf, London, 2003
The four levels of accommodation start at the first floor, which includes a green space for the residents. Public circulation to the flats is external, with a single staircase serving all floors and providing access to the central deck access at each level. A lift is provided at the southern end of the block.

ALBION WHARF

The conspicuous glazed volume, which houses the luxury private flats of Foster and Partners' Albion Riverside, have become a prominent landmark on the River Thames, in full view from London's Chelsea Embankment.

Stephen Archer describes how this signature building contrasts with, and is reinforced by, a new block of affordable housing, also by Fosters, for the Peabody Trust.

On the south bank of the River Thames in Battersea, opposite Cheyne Walk in London's Chelsea, Foster and Partners has recently completed a large, mixed-use development. Located immediately next to the practice's own offices, the development includes commercial, private residential and affordable housing elements. The site, developed by Hutchison Whampoa, was originally home to run-down/derelict warehousing and was a common dumping ground where cars were often set alight. This much neglected area of central London was in stark contrast to the wealthy and fashionable district directly across the river. Fosters proposed a clear regeneration strategy for this derelict riverside area and, hopefully, this intervention will provide some impetus to the regeneration of the wider southern riverside area that includes the, seemingly abandoned, Battersea Power Station.

The overall site diagram was initially developed in consultation with Space Syntax[1] to ensure maximum benefit of the site for both its occupants and London as a whole. The company's research and investigation concluded that new routes and pathways would enable the site to open itself up, not only to residents, but also to the many people who enjoy walking along the banks of the Thames. The main, and most dominant, element of the scheme is Albion Riverside, a large block of flats and penthouses for private sale. This large, free-form building is placed adjacent to the towpath along the water's edge. The Space Syntax findings also led to the residential accommodation being raised up to allow for distinct sight lines and pedestrian pathways, as well as ground-level activities, including transparent restaurant and retail space now bisected by an inviting walkway.

However, while the site is ordered around this main organic block, the smaller elements that restrain it are integral to the success of the whole development. To the south and west lie two, more discreet, rectilinear buildings. The southern one is now occupied as offices for Hutchison Whampoa, and the western structure, Albion Wharf, is a block of affordable flats for the Peabody Trust.

The Peabody Trust is a major provider of social and affordable housing in the London area, which began life as a philanthropic charity in the mid-19th century. Now a housing association, it owns or manages nearly 20,000 housing units, and is committed to the provision of good homes for those who cannot afford to buy independently: 'It's our aim to be one of the country's foremost development and community regeneration agencies, an outstanding landlord and a first-class organisation and social business. To this end, we work with local communities, the Greater London Authority, local government and a wide range of voluntary, private and public sector partners. Our mission? To improve the quality of housing and life for our residents, to tackle social exclusion and to build lasting, sustainable communities.'[2]

Under the leadership of Dickon Robinson, the trust has a sustained history of commissioning high-quality new developments, both in terms of the architecture and innovative planning/construction solutions, and in terms of the tenure for the prospective residents. Examples include Murray Grove, in Hackney, by Cartwright Pickard, and Raines Court, in Stoke Newington, by Alford Hall Monaghan Morris.

Thus, the Albion Wharf block of affordable flats, designed by Foster and Partners, had a tough reputation

to live up to. The design itself had to incorporate many variables: position on the site; budgetary constraints; and the number of units that could be provided after discussions with both the Peabody Trust and the local authority.

At the time of the design process, in 1996, the number of social/affordable units that needed to be provided in large-scale developments was a smaller percentage than is now considered appropriate. However, with a total of 196 domestic units in the Albion Riverside building, the provision of 42 affordable apartments in Albion Wharf comes in at roughly 20 per cent – a very reasonable figure. The position on the site

was more of a sticking point. From both a planning and 'quality' perspective, the area of the site allocated to the housing association was initially perceived as being less than favourable.

Situated beside two very undistinguished buildings – a system-clad mirror-glass block to the west and a poor, suburban-style brick apartment block to the north, the new affordable housing building went through many iterations in mass and plan form before the finished design took shape. Several different plan arrangements were examined, but in the end the most

Below
The clean lines and high quality of the internal finishes lift the interior
of the flats from the merely serviceable to the highly desirable.

straightforward won the day. The architects wanted to provide the optimum solution for their clients so, although river views were greatly restricted, they were maximised. Also maximised were the other views from the site, which, although they do not have the impact of the river frontage, do offer glimpses of life in the area and as such anchor the residents to the wider district in which they find themselves.

As with the larger, private residential block, the decision was taken to raise the accommodation, leaving the ground floor for retail space and the entrance to the residents' underground car park (though this provides parking only for the residents of Albion Riverside, with no provision for the residents of Albion Wharf). This solution provides many benefits, such as increased security and privacy, but also allows the space between the buildings to take on a real sense of being a public space, 'a place of repose'. Here, Fosters has created an outdoor space that emulates the piazzas of Italy.

The language of the smaller block is in stark contrast to its more affluent neighbour, but this does not mean that it was regarded as the 'poor relation' – it is a well-designed and well thought out project. While having a very different agenda, the care and detail of the Peabody building is just as complete. It uses a preformed shuttering system, from Germany, that is attached to the structural frame and then filled with concrete, a construction process that was quick and easy. The combined entrance doors and glazing arrived on site as completed units, as did the full-height glazing and external cladding to the living areas.

ALBION WHARF	G 0-29%	F 30-39%	E 40%	D 41-49%	C 50-59%	B 60-69%	A 70-100%
QUALITATIVE							
Space-Interior						B	
Space-Exterior						B	
Location					C		
Community						B	
QUANTITATIVE							
Construction Cost					C		
Cost-rental/purchase			E				
Cost in use				D			
Sustainability			E				
AESTHETICS							
Good Design?						B	
Appeal							A
Innovative?					C		

This table is based on an analytical method of success in contributing to a solution to housing need. The criteria are: Quality of life – does the project maintain or improve good basic standards? Quantitative factors – has the budget achieved the best it can? Aesthetics – does the building work visually?

One of the perennial issues for any housing project is the provision of storage space (and this scheme is no exception), alongside the debate as to whether or not balconies should be provided. Historically, the combination of limited storage and a balcony has led to the latter becoming an open-air cupboard/ bike store/larder. To prevent this somewhat unsightly evolution, it was decided that balconies would not be provided in the Peabody project and, instead, a large ground-floor bike store would be incorporated, at ground level. However, the glazing to the living spaces does include large French sliding doors with external balustrades, which means that while there may not be an external space, the rooms can still be opened to the outside. The interiors of the flats can, if they wish, become an integral part of the public square beyond.

Laid out as two boxes of differing sizes, the internal planning of Albion Wharf, providing a mix of one- and two-bedroom flats, is clear and legible. The open-plan living space and kitchen are on the outside edge of each block, with the bedrooms and bathrooms on the inner. It is this inner space, between the two blocks, that brings the scheme to life. As with any residential project, public circulation is critical to its success and, here, a variation of 'deck access' provides privacy as well as a sense of community. A central, open-air void between each of the blocks has a single platform running its full length, at each level. These are not, however, immediately outside the front doors of the flats (which could lead to noise pollution – especially at night). Each individual dwelling is separated from the walkway by a bridge, so the boundary to each property begins at the junction of the bridge and the central passage. To emphasise the transition from public to semiprivate, the width of the bridges is greater than that of the platforms. The reality for the residents is that they now have what is almost a garden path, as nearly all the bridges have been furnished with seating and potted plants.

The internal finishes are of a very high standard, with the kitchens and bathrooms particularly well completed. In fact, Peabody decided to install a higher standard of finish here than is the norm for such a project, to ensure that the high standard of the building was not let down by inferior-quality materials.

With such unprepossessing neighbours to the west and north, the views out from the living spaces could have been less than enjoyable. Thus, in the planning stages, it was agreed early on to provide the accommodation in two blocks of unequal length. This planning strategy ensures that while most of the flats have an oblique river view, there are other interesting views in and around the site. It also allows for the inclusion, at first-floor level, of a lawned area for the sole use of the residents, which sits above the entrance to the underground garage mentioned earlier.

The tenure of the building is completely shared ownership, with the occupiers a mix of residents from the borough of Wandsworth and those on the Peabody Trust's own waiting list. The properties were valued at around £240,000 for the one-bedroom apartments and £400,000 for the two-bedrooms. With the initial percentage of each purchase being between 45 and 50 per cent of the market value, these are not cheap homes and, while they do enable some people to get onto the property ladder, low-income key workers such as hospital porters could not afford to buy at these prices. In addition, the maximum stake in their homes that residents will ever be able to achieve is 75 per cent, ensuring that the trust will always have a healthy interest in each property. Maintenance is carried out by Peabody and is financed by an annual service charge levied on the residents.

Overall, from a design perspective, this is a very successful and well thought through development. The different elements work well as a larger composition, with the exuberance of Albion Riverside held in check and enhanced by the calmer language of the flanking buildings. The separation of the social element from the main residential building, on a less attractive section of the site, does raise the question of stigmatisation. However, there are many arguments both for and against this strategy; for example, space standards[3] can be quite different, and management and maintenance by the registered social landlord can be performed more easily if there is separation. But at Albion Wharf, any issues of social exclusion have been skilfully avoided.

Despite the fact that the two aspects of the housing market are in two very different buildings, this separation is a dynamic and positive one. The differing architectural styles complement each other and, certainly, Albion Riverside would lose a lot of its impact had it not such a dialogue with its restrained neighbour. The much talked about, but never really succinctly defined, term 'added value' does actually have meaning here. A run-down, brownfield site in the heart of London is being transformed into a vibrant, well thought out, mixed-use urban quarter fulfilling many of the issues and requirements of the current government's thinking on cities and housing. ᐃ+

Notes

1 Space Syntax is a London-based research company that investigates the way public space is perceived and inhabited by those who use it. Its aim is to help architects see beyond their own design and envisage the wider impact and further possibilities of their work.
2 www.peabody.org.uk.
3 The minimum space standards required by housing associations and the public sector have been legislated for, while in the private sector these minimum requirements do not exist and space provision is determined by the return on investment for the developer. This can lead to planning problems when both elements are combined in a single block.

Stephen Archer is director of London-based Archer Architects, which specialises in the design of social housing. He is currently writing, with Bruce Stewart, *The Architect's Navigation Guide to New Housing*, which is due to be published in spring 2006.

Angel Meadows, Manchester, entry for the New Sustainable Communities
'Energy Revolution' competition, 2004
Section of a mixed-use building showing shared roof surfaces with,
for example, office and exhibition spaces providing gardens for family
apartments above.

PIERCY
CONNER

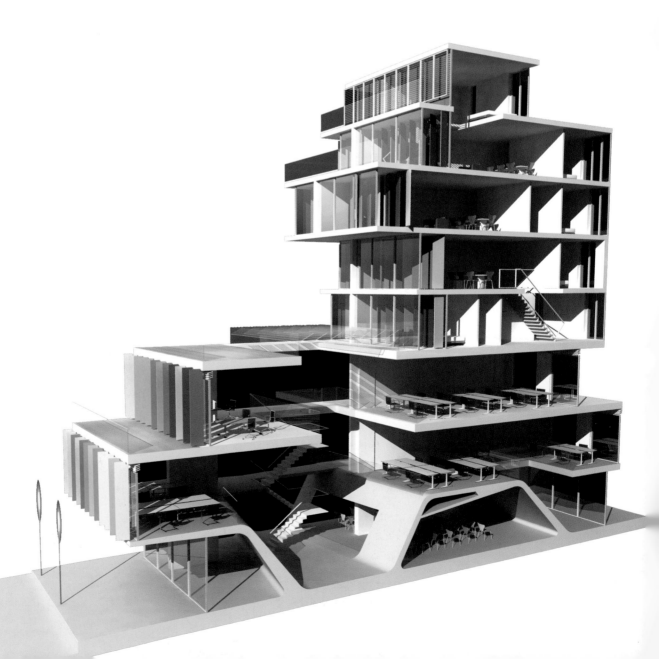

Microflats, view of facade from street on notional Old Street site, east London
The 23-square-metre Microflats are intended to give young workers somewhere affordable to live in the inner city. The blocks are flexible enough in design to be shoehorned into small, dense sites. The modular flats have a striking appearance: sitting in rotated positions in a building frame, they contain utility pods constructed off site, which are plugged together, giving access to external balconies, shower room, storage and services.

Piercy Conner first came to broader public attention with its prototype for the Microflat. Displayed in the windows of Selfridges on London's Oxford Street, it ignited discussions in the press about means of realising affordable urban housing. Lucy Bullivant describes this young practice's enduring commitment to high-density public-housing solutions and the work it has undertaken in communication techniques.

'The future of urban architecture is about inventing new building types that respond to culture, demographics, technology and the changing patterns of our lives,' claim the young London architectural practice Piercy Conner. Since Stuart Piercy and Richard Conner launched the firm in London in 1999, after five years working in Nicholas Grimshaw's office, they have been proactive in proposing architectural concepts that intelligently tackle the needs of society. Many of them constitute new urban models; not so many of them have been built – in part due to a fear of innovation on the part of planners and investors dogging contemporary architecture in the UK. This is not for want of trying, armed as the firm is with an arsenal of propositions that radically rethink housing typologies. The practice has also pioneered ideas in off-site manufacture and investigated simple and easy-to-construct methods of adapting existing low-rise houses as well as converting historic structures for domestic use.

The practice received a slew of public attention for its housing competition entries in the first few years of its life, which demonstrated how consistently keen it was to design new high-density public-housing solutions. The emphasis on customisable design based on innovative finance and delivery equations put Piercy Conner ahead of its time. It even elicited comments from within the architectural world, implying that its marketing techniques were more advanced than its design skills. This is a common syndrome, which obliges young practices not exposed to plentiful commissions to prove otherwise, putting them on the defensive. Now, however, Piercy Conner is finally beginning to enjoy its hard-won credibility.

The practice's vision of design and construction working for mutual advantage is ahead of UK investors' and planners' mindsets, which remain largely conservative. As a result, it does not pitch to the conservative house builders, preferring housing associations, a focus that has led to success with the firm's design for the FLO (Flexible Living Opportunities) House (2000). The FLO project uses off-site manufacturing, and actually won first prize in a competition for houses that can adapt over a lifetime. Circle 333, one of the largest and most adventurous housing associations in the UK, and organiser of the competition, took it to planning for a 36-unit housing development in Wood Green, north London. However, the funding body was concerned about the proposed construction techniques (stressed skin plywood on a CNC-cut timber frame) and the project was never realised.

Although this particular project ground to a halt, the practice captured public imagination with Microflat. This proposal, for high-quality prefabricated housing, was intended to tackle the shortage of suitable affordable properties for young key workers in city centres, and respond to escalating inner-city house prices. Resulting from a hybrid of traditional and factory-made construction, Microflat is a modular design. Each flat is about 32.5 square metres, with a 2.8-metre-high ceiling. The frame of the building is constructed similarly to a standard concrete flat-slab office building, but with utility pods – for the kitchen, dining room (including a small door to an external terrace), shower room and storage – pre-made and inserted into capped services and connected, with a facade element clipped to the concrete frame. The flats are designed to be well insulated, and use recycled materials and solar-heated water almost removing the need for heating. London Housing Federation forecasts show that 80 per cent of the increase in households by 2016 are likely to be in single-person properties, and that by 2011, 40 per cent of London's households will be occupied by only one person.

Reminding people that architects can be entrepreneurs, Piercy Conner's modular design concept was displayed at full size, occupied by volunteer

Top
Microflats, 2002 Visualisation of the Microflat's envelope and balcony showing the design's compact accommodation of facilities.

Middle
Sectional 3-D study model of a single Microflat.

Bottom left
Visualisation of design for a block of 60 Microflat modular units, Old Street,

east London. Piercy Conner speculatively designed a number of alternative blocks of Microflats for different locations in London and Manchester, some hemmed in and others facing main roads.

Bottom right
Visualisation of Microflat's modular design configured for a relatively high-profile site on Kennington Park Road, south London.

inhabitants, in the windows of Selfridges department store in 2002.

The practice began looking for a backer, as well as suitable small, interstitial sites – for example, on the roof above a supermarket. Now there is interest from a local council body that realises that a small-housing policy is necessary in a city like London. Piercy stresses that the units need to be accompanied by provision for diverse facilities at street level to create an intensity of use and interaction. 'Microflats are a pragmatic solution to stem the migration of young city dwellers to the urban periphery,' he says, acknowledging the nub of the resistance to the scheme: that planning procedures need simplifying. 'Planning authorities refer to policy

Top left
Brooks Road Estate low-rise housing competiton entry, Plaistow, London, 2003
A RIBA-run competition to adapt Brooks Road, a dilapidated 1960s housing estate
in Newham, provoked Piercy Conner to consider ways of increasing the flexibility
of the housing and its accessibility to a central urban square, adding a new street.

Bottom left
The design proposed extending each of the existing buildings with a
modular ground-to-roof 'overcoat' – a lightweight steel structure – to
create a new one-bedroom flat at attic level and create more space at
first-floor level.

Top right
Plan showing the spatial impact of the new elevation with its space-
adding 'overcoat' structure.

documents that rarely reflect current demographic and
population change, but which are five to ten years out of date,
though some London boroughs are now updating their policies.'

Relatively few architects have designed houses as products,
especially with the customisable interiors of Microflats. Their
design promotes flexible configurations in the form of several
massing options depending on site conditions. In their
speculative development of new housing typologies based on a
cubic metre measurement and anticipating microsolutions, the
architects agree that there are similarities between their work
and the intentions behind the American Case Study houses. In
the context of the 21st century's urban demographic shifts,
especially in London and other major UK cities, the Microflat
represents excellent potential for the micro-generation of
urban life. Although not yet realised, the whole exercise has
stimulated public thinking about alternative possibilities for
living spaces and their manufacture. The London-based
chairman of the Yo Sushi chain of sushi restaurants recently
invited the practice to evolve a sleeping-pod hotel inspired by
the concept of a retractable bed-chair.

The advantages of prefabrication are that 'it gives you the
pieces to develop, and gets results quickly in a team approach',
say the architects. 'This way, construction allows us to envelop

the space. It doesn't dictate what the building is going
to look like. The key is mass customisation, or the
shaping of a space using mass-produced processes.'
Such processes are already working in fashion, says
Piercy, so why not in architecture? He points out that
the world-famous jeans manufacturer Levi's now offers
a custom-cut jeans service by entering a person's
measurements at a cost little more than the standard
sizes of trouser model.

Countering any impression of the pair as a couple of
architectural innocents, Piercy adds that working at
Grimshaw's instilled in them the importance of the
design process and also taught them how to work on
very large projects. It is clear that they have inherited
some of Grimshaw's interest in use of materials – in
particular, the use of light-steel structures. However,
they take the formal resolution of their architecture to
another stage via their 3-D modelling techniques.
Crucially they are focused on an architecture that is
assembled rather than constructed. For their Martello
Tower (2004–5) on England's Suffolk coast, an old
defensive fort from the early 19th century converted for
residential use, they created a lightweight steel and
laminated plywood roof structure to ensure minimal
visual impact on the setting – an area of natural beauty
– yet offer views from its top. By evolving a detailed 3-D
model, the architects removed from the process the
usual limitations in the fabrication of complex forms by
unfolding the roof into 2-D cutting patterns. Following
manufacture in Hull, in the north of England, as a small
kit of parts, the components were delivered to the site
and assembled there. The roof sits on V-shaped
columns, anchored into the 3-metre-thick brick walls,
floating above the existing parapet of the tower. A 700-
millimetre skirt of frameless curved glass below the
roof provides a spectacular 360-degree view of the
landscape and the sea. 'We tried to derive the 3-D form
from the shape of the monument,' explains Piercy.
English Heritage regards the solution as exemplary,
sensitive to its setting.

One factor that gives Piercy Conner an advantage
over many practices content with designing individual
structures is that the architects have learned to
broaden their perspective on urban contexts. 'Now our

Top left
Martello Tower conversion, Suffolk coast, England, 2004–5
Detail of the tower's new roof sitting on V-shaped columns secured into the brick walls. Curved glazing provides a spectacular 360-degree view of the surrounding landscape and sea.

Middle left
The tower's new roof being fabricated in a workshop in Hull, directly from a 3-D CAD model, and being reassembled on site in position atop the tower parapet.

Bottom left
3-D rapid prototype test model of the roof.

Below
Converted for residential use, the tower, seen across a flood defence and salt-water lake, has a new steel and plywood roof that appears to 'float' above the 3-metre-thick walls and a skirt of frameless glass above the tower's parapet.

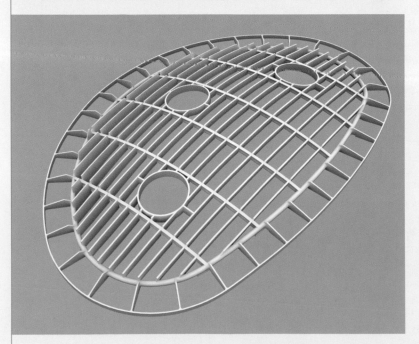

thinking is much more about the bigger picture,' about how design can help to regenerate cities, especially inner-city sites rather than peripheral ones. 'We believe urban sustainability is as much to do with discovering new, economically viable, mixed-use relationships as it is about saving energy,' they say.

The firm's interest in the sustainable future of city dwelling is borne out by the Angel Meadows scheme it submitted to open competition (with Levitt Bernstein and Whitby Bird). The proposal, by the Cooperative Insurance Society (CIS) backed by the INREB Faraday Partnership, was for a new £25 million sustainable community on one of the CIS-owned disused tracts of land in inner Manchester – Angel Meadows, a brownfield site, formerly a car park. 'The postindustrial landscape of the expanding periphery of our cities features void spaces that need to be stitched into the expanding urban fabric,' argue the architects.

The plan aimed to transform Angel Meadows into a sustainable urban community with a mix of building

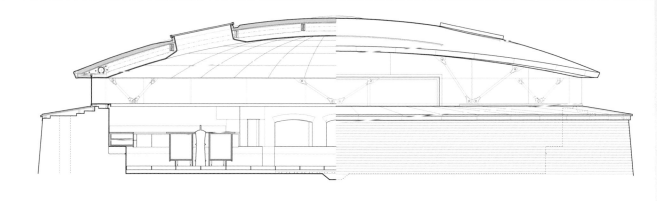

Section elevation of the gently curved roof.

types, including live/work facilities. As the competition did not provide a brief, the architects had to write one, and for them the main challenge was to question what the vague, much bandied-about phrase 'sustainability' really is. In centring the proposal around a mix of uses, rather than purely energy-saving criteria, they identified all the various uses, and dependencies, likely to constitute a feasible programme of 'urban evolution' – a phrase they prefer to 'sustainability'. The emphasis is on family-sized units and giving a dual function to all open areas, countering the inflexible nature of the city's squares. Based on a concept of 'shared surfaces', all the roof surfaces are rendered usable, with office and exhibition areas providing gardens for the family accommodation on the floor above.

Placed second in this competition, Piercy and Conner, still in their early thirties, are coming closer to winning the larger-scale commissions that will allow them to build their concepts. It is to be hoped that competition entries that are never realised at least prove to be a salutary experience. The 2003 RIBA-run competition the practice won for a £12 million adaptation of the 1960s Brooks Road Estate in Plaistow, east London, has proved to be so. In response to the local council's brief, Piercy Conner posed the rhetorical question: 'Is demolition the only solution for London's low-rise housing estates for local borough councils looking for ways to regenerate neighbourhoods under their control?'

Brooks was an estate 'with crime issues, and not very flexible housing', as Piercy puts it, and so it was important to encourage a sense of community ownership. Studying the potential relationship of the houses with the street, in order to find ways in which a secure place to park, promenade and play could be introduced, the architects proposed a modular 'overcoat' – a gently folded form with a modern bay window – that would provide a means of extending the houses with a one-bedroom flat at attic level, or an extra room at first-floor level. Acting as a framework, the overcoat would create a space that could generate a new street focus as well as offer new living spaces.

'As with most affordable housing projects, we look for ways to add value,' comments Piercy. This opportunity to create 36 one-bedroom flats in the roof space by using the roof space of each existing house on the estate seemed by far the best option to 'get a decent-sized building', he continues, giving owners more scope for varied activities within the home. Furthermore, the flats could be sold by the council to create revenue for the landscape and cover overall design and construction costs. The design is a lightweight steel frame, weathered to the existing roof so that it does not touch it, and

is customisable, allowing varying storey heights and roof pitch angles. It operates as an environmental buffer, improving insulation, creating solar energy, collecting rainwater and reusing clean warm air. Conceived in various colours and materials based on options offered by manufacturer Abet Laminati, such a design provides a simple, nonintrusive adaptation to existing low-rise homes, reworking their facades in a way that opens them up to the street. Frustratingly for the architects, the local council lost the courage to see it through, and the project went no further.

After a spate of well-placed competition entries in the last few years – among them Ideal Home's Concept House in 2000, St Mary's Island Housing in London, MFI's Room to Grow and the Unite Affordable Housing Initiative – it must have come as some relief to Piercy Conner when they were commissioned by Derwent Valley to design a £1.5 million housing block on Percival Street in Islington, and another residential scheme further out, in Edmonton, for Country & Metropolitan.

Derwent Valley is a progressive UK developer whose managing director Simon Silver has made it his business to engage many younger architects over the last 15 years, including Troughton McAslan and, more recently, Allford Hall Monaghan Morris. The Islington site is a relatively dense one that has been master-planned into a collection of small areas intended to be exploited for their accommodation opportunities by young architects testing out ideas, in some cases building their first schemes. Piercy Conner's Percival Street housing block is oriented towards the sun and avoids overlooking other apartments. It has a perforated copper facade on the main road that will age and gently patinate, and the side facade is a series of rhythmic bands of glazed sliding screens that filter light into big flexible spaces with high ceilings, creating visible movement – vertical architectural and body patterns – a striking and recurrent feature of the facade.

From the outset, Piercy Conner has been a practice very aware of the potential of architectural representation, an issue many practices are keen to experiment with. A notable feature of its history is the early gestation of Smoothe, a 'design communication' (producing computer visualisations for other architects and for developers) company that operates from its studio in London, as well as from the practice's second office in Manchester. Smoothe quickly became the subsidising force for the practice's speculative work.

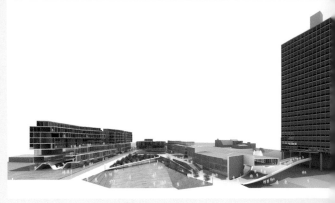

The architects' competence in architectural representation is a two-fold phenomenon, as it is linked to their favoured methods of advanced material organisations, which, in turn, facilitate a transparency in making procedures. By designing all of their projects using 3-D software, spaces and materials can be shaped in discussion with clients, who are now used to seeing full-colour printouts of the firm's rapid prototyping models. The architects favour this test-bed approach, where a design is speculatively presented to the client body or group, and believe it also leads to a more refined form: 'The 3-D testing process allows us to create many hundreds of

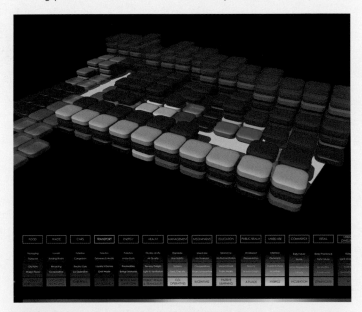

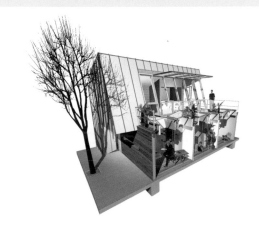

iterations of our concepts.' They have recently become very interested in crafting forms evolved from an analysis of environmental influences. This has included a proposal for a new teaching facility at Leeds Metropolitan University in conjunction with the London- and Manchester-based practice Ian Simpson Architects, in which the surfaces of the building respond to the movements of the sun and patterns of solar heat gain.

The messages Piercy Conner projects are compelling ones, concerning the complex processes to be undertaken to facilitate the evolution of urban environments; and relatively easy for the layman to grasp, if the practice continues to utilise its communication techniques well. They are also timely. The UK government's £22 billion Sustainable Communities scheme, launched in 2003, and its earlier (1997) Millennium Communities programme to nurture sustainable communities, for which the Greenwich Millennium Village has been the 'flagship', demonstrate attempts to cohere the many layers of thinking concerning mixed tenure and higher density. More of this is required.

The Angel Meadows competition has brought some compensations for Piercy Conner. CIS, the client, has endorsed the firm's research-based approach by staging follow-up talks about the 'relationship and dependency chart' the architects evolved for the scheme, which is based on sustainable uses for the site that contrast with the customary 'single use per site' approach. Elsewhere, they are breaking the £2-million-pound barrier in new commissions, including one in the city of London. Making a name for themselves has meant staying true to their innovative principles for design and construction, which offer a fertile seedbed of new ideas. If the UK's urban-regeneration campaigns are to move from good intentions to genuine achievements, they could gain advantage by buying into the work of a credible research-led practice like Piercy Conner. However, local governments and agencies need to be prepared to fight to reinvent planning and investment models for the 21st century and at the same time avoid realising a merely diluted version of their visions. Δ+

PIERCY CONNER

RESUMÉ

Founded in London in 1999
by Richard Conner and Stuart Piercy

Richard Conner and Stuart Piercy

MAJOR WORKS

2000
- FLO (Flexible Living Opportunities) House design development for Circle 333
  (first place, Velux Lifetime Housing Design Competition)

2002
- Microflat installation, Selfridges department store, London
- Studio fit-out and furniture design for Smoothe, Piercy Conner's sister company, London

2003
- £50-million project bid: dwellings, training centre and sports centre development for Bovis Lend Lease
- Retail and office redevelopment, High Holborn, London, for Derwent Valley
- Mixed-use residential development of 40 units, bar and restaurant, for Commonwealth Partners
  (feasibility study), Southwark, London
- Conversion of a Grade II listed stables building, Wales, designed by Sir Clough Williams-Ellis,
  into the Brechfa Fishing Lodge
- Brooks Road Estate, low-rise housing competition, Plaistow, London, for Newham Council (first place)
- Finalist, Building Design/Corus British Steel's International Young Architect of the Year Award

2004
- Mixed-use master plan with 500 residential units for Country & Metropolitan
- INREB New Sustainable Communities 'Energy Revolution' competition, Angel Meadows, Manchester,
  (second place)
- £3-million residential development of 35 units, London, and 40-unit residential development for
  Country & Metropolitan
- £1.5-million residential development of 20 units, Islington, London, for Derwent Valley
- Mixed-use redevelopment, London, for Pearl & Coutts
- £2.5-million residential development and refurbishment of 30 units, LSD Housing Association
- £275,000 conversion of Martello tower scheduled monument, Suffolk coast, England
- Microflat design development, The Microflat Company
- Spa and sauna house, South Wales, for private client
- 250-room hotel, Clifton Street, City of London, for Paul Street Holdings

McLean's Nuggets

Victoria Watson, Cosmological Hop, 2005
Fluctuating magnetism in the emerald–blue spectrum.

Colou(th)read

In engineering there is an increasing use of colour in finite element analysis (FEA) and computational fluid dynamic (CFD) models. The colour is used to illustrate structural forces in FEA modelling and environmental forces such as airflow, smoke spread, water turbulence, acoustics and light in CFD modelling. And in the case of CFD modelling, the graphic output is sufficiently more legible (for architects) than detailed algebraic output from the Navier Stokes equation. Just as when studying the structural forces at work in an acrylic form with a photo-elastic model using polarising filters, hitherto invisible but mathematically describable forces are made visible. We can also read colour as a health indicator with thermochromic thermometers, where colour replaces or augments number. To what extent this new information will start to design our environment remains to be seen. Dr Victoria Watson

Watson explores delaminated woven structures where space, colour and other delights are held in a Cartesian *Farbenfeld* of acrylic fibres. These 'cotton grids' propose a new mode of working for the designer and an exploration of chromatics through a novel approach to the deployment of colour across a three-dimensional environment

(University of Westminster) designs with colour. She explores delaminated woven structures where space, colour and other delights are held in a Cartesian *Farbenfeld* of acrylic fibres. These 'cotton grids' propose a new mode of working for the designer and an exploration of chromatics through a novel approach to the deployment of colour across a three-dimensional environment. *Light and Colour in the Environment*, by Belgian physicist Marcel Minnaert, originally published in 1940, is still one of the few books that specifically explores light and colour as physical phenomena and not theory. Through a series of uncomplicated experiments and observational exercises, blue skies, double rainbows, corona and shadows are enjoyed and explained. To complete the sensorial spectra comes Chicago chef Homaru Cantu's multicoloured menus printed via modified inkjets of fruit and vegetable onto soya-bean and potato-starch paper, which as well as listing the specials of the day at his Moto restaurant are literally good enough to eat.

**Bruce McLean and William McLean, initial drawing for
Blackpool South Promenade prism project, 2002**
Diagram of original prism layout for projected spectrum.

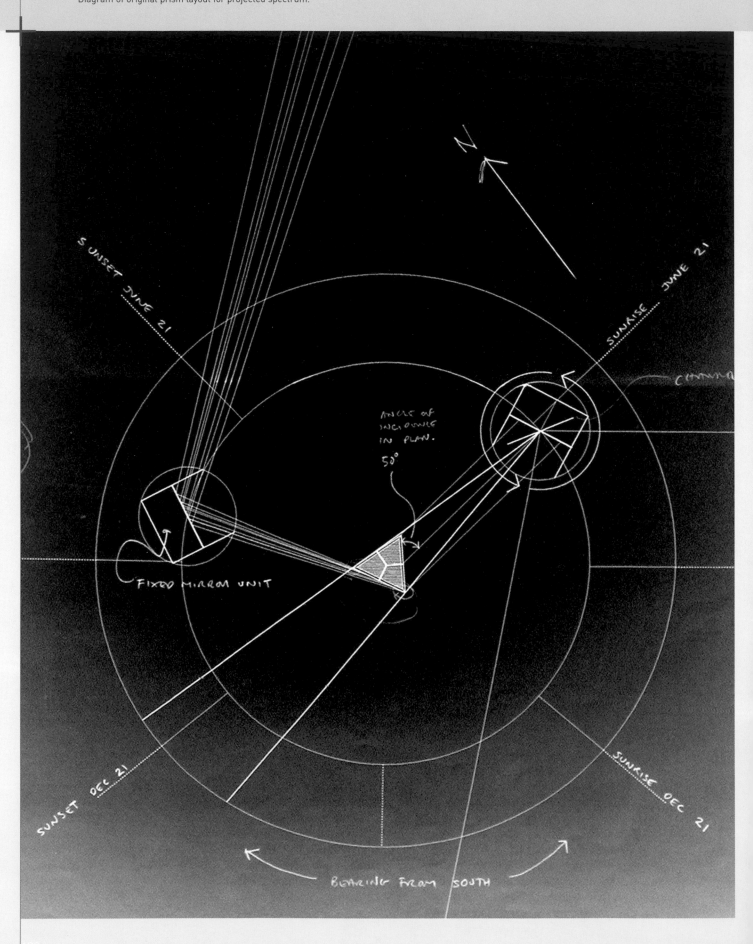

Some Light

Architecture's painfully slow progress should encourage architects to spend more time looking at (not into) the sun. This clock in the sky, which we orbit around in our elliptical way, is nothing if not predictable and a very durable source of energy. In the case of west Austrian Rattenburg, the crystal-glass making village has a very practical/physiological problem, which is lack of sunshine due to its chasmic setting. From mid-November to mid-February, the village sits in the permanent shadow of the Stadtberg mountain. A project by the Bartenbach Light Laboratory and the University of Innsbruck proposes to fit 30 computer-controlled heliostats (sun-tracking mirrors) half a mile to the north of the village, directing sun to a secondary set of building-mounted reflectors to illuminate this sun-starved canyon. Meanwhile, on Blackpool's South Promenade, artist Bruce McLean, architect

> This machine is designed (after initial investment) to provide a perpetual source of coloured light using Isaac Newton's prism and a 'time-compensated solar compass'. The compass has recently been credited with explaining the heroic annual migration of monarch butterflies from North America to Mexico, which head due south despite the relative movement of sun and earth

Chris Leung, plastics man Kees van der Graaf and myself, are developing a kinetic light machine. This machine is designed (after initial investment) to provide a perpetual source of coloured light using Isaac Newton's prism and a 'time-compensated solar compass'. The compass has recently been credited with explaining the heroic annual migration of monarch butterflies from North America to Mexico, which head due south despite the relative movement of sun and earth. This is a slightly more recent idea than Athanasius Kirchner's phototropic clock, circa 1630, which used the sun-tracking behaviour of the sunflower and an extended frond to tell the time. A useful development of the sunflower clock is ecological designer John-Paul Frazer's passive sun-seeking photovoltaics, which cannot help aligning themselves to the brightest light in the sky, increasing the efficiency of the solar cells and animating a seasonal sensibility.

Stick Together

The development of adhesives in our fabricated world continues to flourish. Sixty-five years later, Aerolite 300, a urea-formaldehyde adhesive originally developed for de Havilland's Mosquito aircraft in 1940, is still in use at Oxford-based timber-mast and spar makers Collars. It is used for laminating sitka spruce in exactly the same way as it was used in Howard Hughes' almost airborne (98-metre wingspan) Spruce Goose of 1947. Silicon-bonded structural glazing has been in use for nearly 30 years. It is 10 years since structural engineer Tim Macfarlane launched his all-glass/all-bonded glass museum extension Broadfield House in Dudley; and the gasket-less fully bonded automotive windscreen has become commonplace. Two-pack epoxy chemical anchors now replace expanding bolts for masonry fixings, and medical sutures are not always stitched and are sometimes stuck. It is estimated that over half the component weight of Boeing's new 787 Dreamliner is resin-based composites, reducing the weight of the aircraft by over 20 per cent, and many of these components are bonded and not mechanically fixed. The big advantages of adhesives for aerospace uses are that different types of materials can be bonded where they could not be welded, and stress distributions are much more evenly spread in adhesive bonding than with mechanical fixing methods, like rivets. For current glue types see: silicon, epoxies, cyanoacrylates (superglue), methacrylates, hot melts, uv and anaerobic adhesives. For future glues see: biomimetically engineered products like the much publicised 'Gecko Tape' from 3M that creates a repositionable bond at a molecular level inspired by the gecko's vertiginous adherence. See also a burgeoning nontoxic sector, which will begin to replace the generally toxic solvents and synthetic resin-based bonding products currently available. Naturally based glues such as cellulose derivative methyl cellulose (wallpaper paste), animal glues made from skin and bone, and casein glues made from soured milk curds will be reappraised; and new natural resins (by-products from plant oils such as sunflower and palm) will establish new 'nontoxic' markets, with material toxicity set to become a big political and legislative issue. ∆+

'McLean's Nuggets' is an ongoing technical series inspired by Will McLean and Samantha Hardingham's enthusiasm for back issues of ∆, as explicitly explored in Hardingham's ∆ issue The 1970s is Here and Now (March/April 2005).

Will McLean is joint coordinator (with Pete Silver) of technical studies in the Department of Architecture at the University of Westminster, and is currently collaborating with artist Bruce McLean and architects David Watts and Irene Farish of North Ayrshire Council on a new primary school under construction in Dalry, Scotland.

THE PEACE HOTEL

Opposite
Sassoon House, Shanghai, China
The Peace Hotel today.

Below
Sassoon House concept
The original concept drawing, published in 1927.

Edward Denison recounts the story of one of Shanghai's modern landmarks, the Sassoon House, now known as the Peace Hotel, which has come to represent the city's early 20th-century heyday.

Landmark buildings are a peculiar anomaly. These unassailable architectural icons assume a role greater than the physical space they delineate, and often define an era in the history of their host. In China, the history of urban landscapes is suffused with iconic structures in the form of temples, pagodas or palaces, but its most cosmopolitan urban environment, Shanghai, had no such need for monumental designs. The evolution of China's gateway was fuelled purely by the pursuit of trade.

It is fitting, therefore, that Shanghai's eponymous and famously affluent merchant and property mogul, Victor Sassoon, should build one of Shanghai's first landmark structures in the 1920s. The history of Sassoon House and its site, formerly the most expensive piece of real estate in China, present a remarkable story that mirrors the fortunes of what was once one of the most profligate cities on earth.

Sassoon was one of Shanghai's economic heavyweights from a long and illustrious family line of Baghdadi Jews who arrived in Shanghai in 1844, the year after the British had invaded China and prised open the empire's previously locked door to trade. Vast fortunes were made in opium and property as the untouchable foreign enclave of Shanghai revelled in economic prosperity, while China wallowed in dynastic decline.

The purchase of the site at the corner of Shanghai's two most eminent streets, the Bund and Nanjing Road, marked the start of the Sassoon family's commercial property portfolio in Shanghai in 1877. East Nanjing Road was then a paltry street; tortuous and narrow due to it being laid over a former creek that flowed into Shanghai's Whuangpu River. By the 1920s, it was the largest shopping street in Asia. With a sharp eye for the property market, in 1926 Sassoon commissioned Palmer & Turner, a Hong Kong architectural firm, to draft plans for the tallest and most sophisticated office building in China, just before Shanghai's largest construction boom until the 1990s. The proposal, prepared by the British architect George Wilson, advocated the demolition of two former buildings occupying the site, so widening Nanjing Road and thereby giving the new building a peculiarly irregular floor plan.

Another problem was caused by Shanghai's alluvial soil, which descends hundreds of metres and deprives buildings of a sufficient foundation. To overcome this problem, from about 1910 reinforced concrete rafts on which buildings could literally float started to be used. The raft supporting Sassoon House's 12-storey structure was 325 x 188 feet, pinned to the ground by a thousand pine piles.

During construction, Sassoon decided that the building's primary function was to be a hotel, so the plans were altered and the Cathay Hotel, formerly among the most lavish hotels in the world, was conceived. Here, guests could soak in solid marble baths filled with spring water flowing from silver taps, while the interior designs of suites facing the Bund, like the city's awkward architectural menagerie, represented a curious concoction of styles including Jacobean, Georgian, Indian, Chinese, Japanese, modern French and ultra-Modern. One suite was even named 'The Coward Suite' after Noël Coward, who had spent four days there writing *Private Lives*. The eighth floor contained the hotel reception and the renowned ballroom that became one of Shanghai's most sumptuous venues. On the top floor, at the base of the distinctive pyramid roof, was Sassoon's private apartment.

Architecturally, Sassoon House marks an important turning point in the history of Shanghai's urban landscape. Located near the centre of the Bund – 'one of the handsomest streets in the world'[1] to some, and 'a long line of pompous toadstools raised by anonymous banks, trusts and commercial firms'[2] to others – this famous quasi-colonial river frontage was dominated by

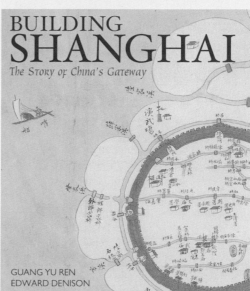

the financial behemoths housed in Neo-Renaissance piles and staid exteriors. The interior and exterior design of Sassoon House was the first to break from tradition by cautiously embracing a modern architectural style, which quickly led to an espousal of Modernism, a style that would later imbue Shanghai. The building's tall, narrow windows and vertical surface detailing convey a refined progressiveness, in contrast to the horizontal configurations of sober solid granite that predominate in its older conservative neighbours. Modern and oriental motifs in low relief were also adopted in granite carvings and bronzework throughout the building, marking a distinct departure from the classical designs that bedeck Shanghai's earlier buildings.

In keeping with being more than just a building, Sassoon House witnessed the start of the Second World War unfolding on its doorstep. On 14 August 1937, following Japan's invasion of China, Chiang Kai-shek's air force attacked the Japanese cruiser, *Idzumo*, moored in the Whuangpu. Two bombs were released too early and smashed into the side of Sassoon House. With the streets awash with Chinese refugees flooding into Shanghai, more than 1,500 people were killed and

wounded in the shadow of Asia's most luxurious hotel. Shanghai's landmark building that symbolised the city's zenith, oversaw also its swift downfall. Today, with Shanghai's resurgence echoing that of the late 1920s, the former Sassoon House, now the Peace Hotel, dishes out nostalgia to eager tourists as the city's new colossal landmarks mushroom from the mudflats and define the current epoch, which is yet to close. ∆+

Notes
1 CE Darwent, *Shanghai: A Handbook for Travellers and Residents to the Chief Objects of Interest in and Around the Foreign Settlements and Native City*, Kelly & Walsh (Shanghai), 2nd edn, 1920, p 4.
2 Harold Acton, *Memoirs of an Aesthete*, Methuen (London), 1948, p 292.

Edward Denison is the author, with Guang Yu Ren, of *Building Shanghai: The Story of China's Gateway*, which is to be published by Wiley-Academy in early 2006. See www.wiley.com for further details.

THE BOOK THAT WOULD BE A CITY

Colin Fournier, Professor in Architecture and Urban Planning at the Bartlett School of Architecture, UCL, and co-architect of the inimitable Kunsthaus Graz, reviews David Grahame Shane's book *Recombinant Urbanism*, which he finds to be 'as complex and exciting, multifaceted and contradictory as the city itself'.

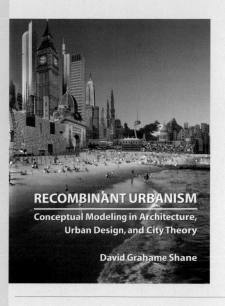

RECOMBINANT URBANISM: CONCEPTUAL MODELING IN ARCHITECTURE, URBAN DESIGN, AND CITY THEORY
David Grahame Shane (Wiley-Academy, 2005)

PB £26.99 ($40.50) and HB £75.00/$112.50
For more details see www.wiley.com

Apart from a few notable exceptions, books on urbanism tend to be disappointing for the fundamental reason that they generally fail to match the extraordinary richness of their subject matter. While the cyberneticians' classic 'law or requisite variety' stipulates that a model of a system under observation must exhibit at least as much internal variety as the system itself, books on urban phenomena tend, often involuntarily, to focus on one aspect or one interpretation of the city, and therefore quickly lose their relevance as explanatory models.

Dr Grahame Shane has managed the *tour de force* of producing a book on urbanism that is as complex and exciting, multifaceted and contradictory as the city itself. By a remarkable process of mimetic appropriation of its subject matter, the book appears to have taken on many of the intrinsic attributes of the city. So accomplished is its ability to uncover different models of the city that it becomes, in effect, a true embodiment of the city.

Since the end of Modernism, Shane argues, the city no longer has a master plan, no one is in control; and in a very challenging way this remarkable book also relinquishes conventional notions of literary control, becoming instead a recombinant organism, a self-organising system capable, like the urban realm, of harbouring a multiplicity of events and actors. Shane's reading of the city as a complex and ever-changing assemblage of armatures, enclaves and heterotopias – the latter defined as cultural singularities within the city that may come into conflict with their host and eventually take over from it – is precisely the basis of the book's underlying philosophy and structure: it is an assemblage of conceptual heterotopias, models within the model, that grow in parallel as the book unfolds and freely compete with each other.

Not unlike Jorge Luis Borges' urban metaphor in *The Library of Babel*, the book effectively contains everything you ever wanted to know about urban design, every theory, the refutation of that theory and even the refutation of the refutation. Similarly, the abundant iconography, with over 700 illustrations, appears to include every key image of the city ever published. It constitutes an amazingly compact descriptive microcosm and a powerful critical tool.

These unique qualities could also have been the book's Achilles' heel: complexity and variety of information can lead to implosion, as was the mythic fate of both the tower and library of Babel, but the second *tour de force* of the book is that, as Stuart Kauffman says of complex systems that have evolved successfully, it manages to maintain itself 'on the edge of chaos', loose enough to allow an infinity of re-combinations, but exhibiting enough order to maintain a continuity of meaning and intent.

What gives this book its unique kind of order – its underlying armature, to use Shane's terminology – is that it is grounded in the author's intimate knowledge of various cities around the world and, ultimately, in the values he holds – the fact that the author, without prescribing any simplistic solutions, takes a clear normative stand about the future evolution of the city.

The golden thread throughout the book is the voice of a man who, while totally immersed in the intellectual and design sophistication of Postmodernity, has retained a deeply humanist belief in the cultural, social and political importance of the urban artefact, in the quality of life that the city, whatever form it may take in the future, must continue to offer and sustain. ⌂+

Subscribe Now for 2006

As an influential and prestigious architectural publication, *Architectural Design* has an almost unrivalled reputation worldwide. Published bimonthly, it successfully combines the currency and topicality of a newsstand journal with the editorial rigour and design qualities of a book. Consistently at the forefront of cultural thought and design since the 1960s, it has time and again proved provocative and inspirational – inspiring theoretical, creative and technological advances. Prominent in the 1980s for the part it played in Postmodernism and then in Deconstruction, $\triangle$ has recently taken a pioneering role in the technological revolution of the 1990s. With groundbreaking titles dealing with cyberspace and hypersurface architecture, it has pursued the conceptual and critical implications of high-end computer software and virtual realities. $\triangle$

$\triangle$ Architectural Design

SUBSCRIPTION RATES 2006
Institutional Rate (Print only or Online only): UK£175/US$290
Institutional Rate (Combined Print and Online): UK£193/US$320
Personal Rate (Print only): UK£99/US$155
Discount Student* Rate (Print only): UK£70/US$110

*Proof of studentship will be required when placing an order. Prices reflect rates for a 2005 subscription and are subject to change without notice.

TO SUBSCRIBE
Phone your credit card order:
+44 (0)1243 843 828

Fax your credit card order to:
+44 (0)1243 770 432

Email your credit card order to:
cs-journals@wiley.co.uk

Post your credit card or cheque order to:
John Wiley & Sons Ltd.
Journals Administration Department
1 Oldlands Way
Bognor Regis
West Sussex PO22 9SA
UK

Please include your postal delivery address with your order.

All $\triangle$ volumes are available individually. To place an order please write to:
John Wiley & Sons Ltd
Customer Services
1 Oldlands Way
Bognor Regis
West Sussex PO22 9SA

Please quote the ISBN number of the issue(s) you are ordering.

$\triangle$ is available to purchase on both a subscription basis and as individual volumes

---

○ I wish to subscribe to $\triangle$ *Architectural Design* at the **Institutional rate of (Print only or Online only** *(delete as applicable)* **£175/us$290**.

○ I wish to subscribe to $\triangle$ *Architectural Design* at the **Institutional rate of (Combined Print and Online) £193/us$320**.

○ I wish to subscribe to $\triangle$ *Architectural Design* at the **Personal rate of £99/us$155**.

○ I wish to subscribe to $\triangle$ *Architectural Design* at the **Student rate of £70/us$110**.

○ $\triangle$ *Architectural Design* is available to individuals on either a calendar year or rolling annual basis; Institutional subscriptions are only available on a calendar year basis. Tick this box if you would like your Personal or Student subscription on a rolling annual basis.

Payment enclosed by Cheque/Money order/Drafts.

Value/Currency £/US$ [   ]

○ Please charge £/US$ [   ] to my credit card.
Account number:
[ ][ ][ ][ ][ ][ ][ ][ ][ ][ ][ ][ ][ ][ ][ ][ ]

Expiry date:
[ ][ ][ ][ ][ ][ ]

Card: Visa/Amex/Mastercard/Eurocard *(delete as applicable)*

Cardholder's signature [   ]

Cardholder's name [   ]

Address [   ]
[   ]
[   ] Post/Zip Code [   ]

Recipient's name [   ]

Address [   ]
[   ]
[   ] Post/Zip Code [   ]

I would like to buy the following issues at £22.50 each:

○ $\triangle$ 178 *Sensing the 21st-Century City* Brian McGrath + Grahame Shane

○ $\triangle$ 177 *The New Mix*, Sara Caples and Everardo Jefferson

○ $\triangle$ 176 *Design Through Making*, Bob Sheil

○ $\triangle$ 175 *Food + The City*, Karen A Franck

○ $\triangle$ 174 *The 1970s Is Here and Now*, Samantha Hardingham

○ $\triangle$ 173 *4dspace: Interactive Architecture*, Lucy Bullivant

○ $\triangle$ 172 *Islam + Architecture*, Sabiha Foster

○ $\triangle$ 171 *Back To School*, Michael Chadwick

○ $\triangle$ 170 *The Challenge of Suburbia*, Ilka + Andreas Ruby

○ $\triangle$ 169 *Emergence*, Michael Hensel, Achim Menges + Michael Weinstock

○ $\triangle$ 168 *Extreme Sites*, Deborah Gans + Claire Weisz

○ $\triangle$ 167 *Property Development*, David Sokol

○ $\triangle$ 166 *Club Culture*, Eleanor Curtis

○ $\triangle$ 165 *Urban Flashes Asia*, Nicholas Boyarsky + Peter Lang

○ $\triangle$ 164 *Home Front: New Developments in Housing*, Lucy Bullivant

○ $\triangle$ 163 *Art + Architecture*, Ivan Margolius

○ $\triangle$ 162 *Surface Consciousness*, Mark Taylor

○ $\triangle$ 161 *Off the Radar*, Brian Carter + Annette LeCuyer

○ $\triangle$ 160 *Food + Architecture*, Karen A Franck

○ $\triangle$ 159 *Versioning in Architecture*, SHoP

○ $\triangle$ 158 *Furniture + Architecture*, Edwin Heathcote

○ $\triangle$ 157 *Reflexive Architecture*, Neil Spiller

○ $\triangle$ 156 *Poetics in Architecture*, Leon van Schaik

○ $\triangle$ 155 *Contemporary Techniques in Architecture*, Ali Rahim

○ $\triangle$ 154 *Fame and Architecture*, J. Chance and T. Schmiedeknecht

○ $\triangle$ 153 *Looking Back in Envy*, Jan Kaplicky